Skin Deep:
debating body image

Series Editor: Cara Acred

Volume 234

Independence Educational Publishers

First published by Independence Educational Publishers

The Studio, High Green

Great Shelford

Cambridge CB22 5EG

England

© Independence 2012

British Library Cataloguing in Publication Data

Skin deep : debating body image. – (Issues ; v. 234)

1. Body image.

I. Series II. Acred, Cara.

306.4'613-dc23

ISBN-13: 9781 86168 627 5

Printed in Great Britain

MWL Print Group Ltd

Contents

Introduction

Skin Deep: debating body image is Volume 234 in the **Issues** series. The aim of the series is to offer current, diverse information about important issues in our world, from a UK perspective.

ABOUT SKIN DEEP: DEBATING BODY IMAGE

Today, body image is not only a concern for women; in our media driven, celeb-conscious society, increasing numbers of men, and girls as young as five years old, worry about their body shape and appearance. With the rise of plastic surgery and an airbrushing epidemic sweeping the Net, television and magazine industries, body dysmorphia is becoming an ever more worrying issue. This book explores the causes of negative body image, examines its effects and looks at ways in which we can tackle the problem.

OUR SOURCES

Titles in the **Issues** series are designed to function as educational resource books, providing a balanced overview of a specific subject.

The information in our books is comprised of facts, articles and opinions from many different sources, including:

* Newspaper reports and opinion pieces

* Website fact sheets

* Magazine and journal articles

* Statistics and surveys

* Government reports

* Literature from special interest groups

A NOTE ON CRITICAL EVALUATION

Because the information reprinted here is from a number of different sources, readers should bear in mind the origin of the text and whether the source is likely to have a particular bias when presenting information (or when conducting their research). It is hoped that, as you read about the many aspects of the issues explored in this book, you will critically evaluate the information presented.

It is important that you decide whether you are being presented with facts or opinions. Does the writer give a biased or unbiased report? If an opinion is being expressed, do you agree with the writer? Is there potential bias to the 'facts' or statistics behind an article?

ASSIGNMENTS

In the back of this book, you will find a selection of assignments designed to help you engage with the articles you have been reading and to explore your own opinions. Some tasks will take longer than others and there is a mixture of design, writing and research based activities that you can complete alone or in a group.

FURTHER RESEARCH

At the end of each article we have listed its source and a website that you can visit if you would like to conduct your own research. Please remember to critically evaluate any sources that you consult and consider whether the information you are viewing is accurate and unbiased.

Body image

Information from the University of Dundee Counselling Service.

By Zinaida Lewczuk Ph.D

Introduction

Body image is the subjective sense we have of our appearance and the experience of our physical embodiment. It is built from memories that go back to our childhood. It is also influenced by wider social and cultural standards (viz. The media). In the west the message 'thin is beautiful' carries great power. The result is for women and even quite young girls to be very concerned with the shape and size of their bodies. It can also affect men, though not to the same extent. In this leaflet, we will be dealing with female body image, though some of it will apply to men.

Problems with body image

⇨ Feelings and thoughts. If you have a very poor body image, you are likely to be preoccupied with some features of your appearance. You may wish for different looks, you may compare yourself constantly with others; you may always see yourself in a negative light. Your anxieties will intensify your thoughts and feelings.

⇨ Behaviour. Poor body image can stop you going to parties, doing sports, wearing fashionable clothes, etc. You may even try to disguise the parts of your body you don't like. It may interfere with romantic relationships because you are afraid of another person getting close to you and touching you.

⇨ Self-esteem. Your feelings about your body may become a barometer of how you feel about yourself as a person. Your obsession with your body may make you forget that inside it lives a valuable human being with unique gifts and qualities.

⇨ Blinkers. By making superhuman efforts to give your body the right shape, you may miss other opportunities in life and fail to develop your potential. There is so much futility and waste in hating your body.

⇨ Depression. You may feel so negative about your life and your future prospects because of how you think you look that you become depressed. Common symptoms of depression include low mood, feelings of worthlessness, constant fatigue, sleep problems, lack of appetite, etc.

⇨ Eating disorders. The subjective sense that we have of our appearance often doesn't correspond to our objective shape and size. People with eating disorders usually over-estimate their size, and although they may look normal or thin to an observer they feel quite differently inside.

Persistence of a negative body image

⇨ The myth that 'thin is beautiful' and attainable. The myth goes something like this, 'if only you worked hard enough at dieting and exercising you would be thinner and acquire the right shape'. Buy into this myth and you perpetuate it. Only a minority of women are genetically programmed to continually fall within the narrow weight range of the cultural ideal. For most women the fashionable shape is unattainable. This has always been the case. Every society contrives to promote body images that elude the majority.

⇨ Internalised negative script. Your body image is built up from experiences of how you were cared for as a baby, a toddler and later a child. The messages you received from your parents and peers will have made a difference, and how you used your imagination to make these experiences your own by internalising them. The negative script was created over many years, but it can be changed.

⇨ Fear of change. Any change, even for the better, can be scary. Faced with change we are always tempted to maintain the status quo. Perhaps you used your negative body image to stop you from taking responsibility for making important changes in your life, because they felt risky to you. But in choosing to make no changes, your life can become stuck and mired in your anxieties.

Improving your body image

⇨ Shift your attitude. As one woman put it, 'unless you feel beautiful inside, you will not see your outer beauty, let alone believe or enjoy it'. You can look attractive to others yet feel fat and ugly inside. The inner shift has to come first and it doesn't happen overnight. You need to move from a position of disliking or even hating your body to a position where you are treating yourself with compassion and willing to learn how to appreciate yourself. However awful you may feel about yourself, it is very likely that deep down inside you there is a small voice that wants you to feel better about yourself and your body. Find this voice, listen to it and strengthen it.

'During some eras, today's cellulite was a sign of beauty and health'

⇨ Challenge distorted patterns of thinking.

   ⇨ Emotional reasoning. 'I feel fat, therefore I must be fat.' You are assuming that how you feel reflects how things really are.

   ⇨ All or nothing thinking. 'My thighs are big, therefore I'm totally unattractive.' You see everything in black and white terms.

   ⇨ Discounting the positives. 'I can't stop thinking about my flat chest.' You pick out negative details and dwell on them, and completely ignore all the positive aspects about yourself.

   ⇨ Changing positive feedback into negative thoughts. If somebody says to you, 'You look really well', you might turn it into, 'that means I have put on weight and am getting fat'. Or you might think, 'They're only saying that to please me, they don't really mean it.'

With all of the above, say 'STOP' to yourself and deliberately replace the negative thought with a positive affirming one, even if that feels slightly strange to begin with. Learn to accept and enjoy compliments.

Practice positive affirmations

Affirmations can serve as antidotes to the destructive, toxic messages that you give yourself. They can be a powerful tool for inner transformation and healing. Even if you are disappointed with your body, you need to develop a compassionate way of relating to it, because a change for the better can only follow from greater self-acceptance. For example:

⇨ 'I'm alright just the way I am.'

⇨ 'I like myself.'

⇨ 'My legs are strong and powerful and they work well for me.'

It's even better if you create your own affirmations. The more imaginative and self-affirming the better! Always make them positive: e.g. 'I like myself' rather than 'I don't hate myself.' Repeat them often, place them on cards, stick them around your room, and carry them around. The goal is to deliberately reprogram some of the deep, largely unconscious, wiring that has been causing you so much distress. If you encounter a strong internal resistance to an affirmation, don't give up. Check where it's coming from – there may be important clues as to why you don't yet wish to let go of your negative body image.

Changing your behaviour

List the things that you avoid because of the way you feel about your body. Then put them in order from least feared to most feared. Using this list gradually change your avoidance behaviour. Suppose the least feared is wearing a short-sleeved T-shirt. In spite of feeling self-conscious and anxious, try wearing it on a few occasions, even just keeping it on at home. When it becomes easier, try the next item on the list. You will start to gradually regain your sense of control.

'In China foot binding was considered the height of fashion, resulting in a stump that could hardly be walked on'

Cultural issues related to body image

At different times different female shapes have been fashionable. During some eras, today's cellulite, i.e. dimpled flesh, was a sign of beauty and health. A slim silhouette, so fashionable today, was considered sickly and unattractive. In the 19th century, a tiny waist was in vogue, and to acquire it, women practised squeezing their bodies into corsets, bruising their internal organs and sometimes breaking their ribs. In China foot binding was considered the height of fashion, resulting in a stump that could hardly be walked on. The ideal in fashion is usually difficult to attain, elitist, and highly competitive. It requires time and money. If too many women attain it, then the ideal changes to become elusive once more. Gaining a wider and wiser perspective on the changing ideal of perfect shape and size may give you a more critical view on the absurdities associated with body image. Restricting food intake, worrying about calories, endlessly finding fault with yourself bring little in the way of peace of mind, happiness or fulfilment.

⇨ The above information is reprinted with kind permission from the University of Dundee Counselling Service. Visit www.dundee.ac.uk/counselling for further information on this and other subjects.

Exercises

Our imagination can help us to get in touch with the intuitive and emotional aspects of ourselves more easily than the logical mind. We can use our imagination to take us a step further in our efforts to transform our body image.

In doing the following exercises make sure that you won't be disturbed or interrupted.

Exercise 1

Choose three words or phrases that best describe your negative feelings and attitudes about your body, and write them down on separate pieces of paper.

Arrange the pieces in a pile with the one you identify with most at the bottom. Focus on the top piece of paper. Imagine that it's a kind of garment that you are wearing. Make it as vivid as possible. Notice the colour, shape, texture, etc.

This garment is one of the ways in which you define yourself. Explore how it feels to be defined in this way. What sort of thoughts, sensations, feelings go along with this self-image? Explore how this self-definition affects your self-esteem, your relationships, your peace of mind – in other words how does it limit and affect your whole life?

In your imagination, now take this garment off. Notice how it feels to be without it. Is there a shift in your feelings, sensations and thoughts? Examine what it is like to be without it. What do you gain? What do you lose?

Follow the same steps with the other two pieces of paper, finally of course dealing with the word/phrase that you feel is closest to you. When you have finished, rest quietly for a while before starting some other activity.

In doing this exercise regularly, you can see if you are able to gradually let go of some of your negative self-definitions.

Exercise 2

This involves writing a letter to your body and your body writing back to you. You have two sheets of paper. On the first one, write a letter to your body as though your body were a person. Try to write continuously without censoring anything. Then put this letter aside.

Now close your eyes, take a few deep breaths, and try to identify with your body. In your imagination become your body and experience how it feels to receive the letter. Stay with the experience for a moment or two.

Now using the second sheet let a response from your body form itself in your imagination. Once again don't censor anything. Just write without stopping.

Finally sit quietly for a while and reflect on the exercise. What have you learnt? The purpose of this exercise is to open up a channel of communication between you and your body. Constructive mind-body communication will ease integration, harmony and self-acceptance.

Uncomfortable in our skin: the body image report

More of us than ever hate the way that we look. It's making us anxious, unhealthy and disempowered. A special report on the pressures distorting the way we think and feel.

By Eva Wiseman

Outside, on a warm morning in March, students at the University of the West of England are shading their faces with textbooks, legs rippling in the sun. Inside, in a cramped, bright room lined with ring binders labelled 'Intimacy', the women who make up the world's only Centre for Appearance Research (CAR) are talking quietly about perfection. I arrived here after following a trail of newspaper reports – on the effect of airbrushing in the media, on men's growing anxiety about their weight – reports used variously by politicians and educators to highlight the way our world is collapsing. It's here, with their biscuits and gentle, resigned chatter, that a team led by Professor Nichola Rumsey and Dr Diana Harcourt is compiling the research required to understand how we deal with changing attitudes to appearance, and along the way

helping answer the question: why do we hate the way we look?

Two years ago I started writing a column for a magazine, illustrated by a photo of my face. At times it made me feel odd (I have never liked photos), at other times sad, often anxious. It made me more aware that I don't like the way I look, but more, I don't like the fact that I don't like it. But it's not just me. All CAR's research suggests that Britain's body image is in crisis.

Body image is a subjective experience of appearance. It's an accumulation of a lifetime's associations, neuroses and desires, projected on to our upper arms, our thighs. At five, children begin to understand other people's judgement of them. At seven they're beginning to show body dissatisfaction. As adults 90% of British women feel body-image

anxiety. And it doesn't wane – many women in their 80s are still anxious about the way their bodies look which, Professor Rumsey explains, can even affect their treatment in hospital, when their health choices are influenced by aesthetics. Many young women say they are too self-aware to exercise; many say they drink to feel comfortable with the way they look; 50% of girls smoke to suppress their appetite – is it too strong to suggest that these things, these anxieties, are slowly killing them?

Liberal Democrat MP Jo Swinson (who has succeeded in pulling a number of L'Oréal ad campaigns for being unrealistic) is one of a growing group of people whose campaigning indicates that it's something worth worrying about. Last year I attended every session of her government inquiry into body image, the results of which were published in a report this month. She cited research showing how current 'airbrushing' culture leads to huge self-esteem problems – half of all 16- to 21-year-old women would consider cosmetic surgery and in the past 15 years eating disorders have doubled. Young people, she said, don't perform actively in class when they're not feeling confident about their appearance.

'We don't even know we hate our bodies because we take that for granted'

It is research backed up by a new documentary by Jennifer Siebel Newsom, *Miss Representation*, about the under-representation of women in positions of power – women who are high 'self objectifiers' have low political power. They're less likely to run in politics, and less likely to vote: if value lies in their imperfect bodies, they feel disempowered. The long-term effects, the piling on of pressures one by one, like a dangerous Jenga tower, means women's – and increasingly men's, 69% of whom 'often' wish they looked like someone else – lives are being damaged, not by the way they look but by the way they feel about the way they look. It's complicated.

Even researching such a thing is tricky. The truth feels slippery. 'Why,' I asked the psychotherapist Susie Orbach (who, since publishing *Fat is a Feminist Issue* in 1978, has become a loud and public voice in the conversation about body image), 'when I know that beauty is subjective, that nothing terrible would happen if I put on weight, when my desk is covered in annotated research on bodies, do I still feel bad about the way I look?'

'Because none of us lives in a vacuum,' she said. Simply acknowledging the pressure doesn't eliminate it. 'We don't even know we hate our bodies because we take that for granted.' She sighed. 'When I wrote FiFi there was a pretty bad situation,' she said, 'but the women of my generation have given birth to... this.' To my generation – 60% of whom feel ashamed of how they

look. But before anybody begins to deal with this, this crippling western-worldwide anxiety, it's important to try and work out why. How did we get here?

At the Centre for Appearance Research, they discuss with me how invested people have become in their appearance. And how central it now is to the value they place on themselves. We've always compared ourselves to other people, but what has changed is the way we use images. There's a famous study which looked at teenage girls in Fiji after television was introduced to the island for the first time in 1995. After three years with TV, the girls who watched it the most were 50% more likely to describe themselves as 'too fat'; 29% scored highly on a test of eating-disorder risk. One girl said of the western women she watched on *Beverly Hills 90210*: 'In order to be like them, I have to work on myself, exercising, and my eating habits should change.'

Today the web ensures that we are drowning in visuals: we're no longer comparing ourselves to 'local images' – our friends – instead we're comparing ourselves to social-networked strangers, celebrities, and to Photoshopped images, of which we see around 5,000 a week. I always bristle a little when 'airbrushing' or Photoshop is blamed for the rise of body-image anxiety. It seems too simple. While I was impressed by Jo Swinson's campaign to ban airbrushing in advertising, I did cheer, a little, when I read Tina Fey's thoughts: 'Photoshop itself is not evil,' she wrote. 'Just like Italian salad dressing is not inherently evil, until you rub it all over a desperate young actress and stick her on the cover of *Maxim*, pretending to pull her panties down. Give it up. Retouching is here to stay. Technology doesn't move backward. No society has ever deindustrialised.'

The problem is not the Photoshopping itself – the problem is that Photoshopped images threaten to replace all others, and that in slicing off the rounded hip of an actress it reveals our difficult relationship with the female body. The problem is that, in their ubiquity, Photoshopped

images have changed our standards of comparison. So that's one reason. Images. I started to make a list.

The 'size zero' debate that began a few years ago led to an angry dissection of the fashion industry's preference for skinny models. In response, a circular argument was repeated, laying blame on fashion magazines (for printing the pictures), then model agencies (for hiring the models), then designers (for making samples that only fit the very thinnest of them). In this month's *Vogue*, editor Alexandra Shulman launched the Health Initiative, a six-point pact between the editors of the 19 international editions, aimed at encouraging a healthier approach to body image within the industry. They promise to encourage designers to 'consider the consequences of unrealistically small sample sizes of their clothing, which... encourages the use of extremely thin models'. Is this the industry taking responsibility for our broken body image, for its power? Acknowledging that they help sell not only clothes, but ideas of which bodies are acceptable?

> ## 'The web ensures that we are drowning in visuals: we're no longer comparing ourselves to our friends, instead we're comparing ourselves to social-networked strangers, celebrities, and to Photoshopped images, of which we see around 5,000 a week'

'We're not taking responsibility for it,' Shulman says firmly. 'We're saying we realise we're in a powerful position and we can do something about it.'

We're sitting in her bright white office, beside shelves displaying international *Vogue* covers. She points at them one by one. "There's Kate Moss in Versace. That [sample-sized] dress is tiny. You can see it's pretty tight on her. Then there's Scarlett Johansson in vintage

Prada – you see, "real people", actors as opposed to models, don't fit sample-size clothes.'

Caryn Franklin, Erin O'Connor and Debra Bourne, whose All Walks Beyond the Catwalk initiative encourages diversity in fashion, talk to designers and students about creating more 'inclusive' designs. 'The fashion industry has changed in the past decade,' Franklin explains slowly, trying to put her finger on why our body image is in crisis. 'The catwalk used to be a factory space. But digital changed everything – it's now become a luxury positioning experience, a consumer space.'

It's helpful for fashion buyers (the audience at catwalk shows) to see clothes on a shape that is as close to a clothes hanger as possible – hence the tall, bony models whose breasts will not bother the line of a shirt. But since catwalk imagery has gone mainstream, these model shapes have drifted into the public subconscious. 'We're helping the industry understand this,' adds Franklin. 'This inconvenient truth.'

Shulman has been pushing for larger sample sizes since 2009, when she wrote a letter to major international designers complaining that their tiny designs were forcing editors to shoot them on models with 'no breasts or hips'. Has she seen any change? 'Hmm. There is still a bit of a… blindness. I think fashion is a bit out of step with this. They don't realise that people would really like to see something different.' She's right – Ben Barry (a PhD student at Cambridge University) surveyed 3,000 women, the vast majority of whom 'significantly increase purchase intentions when they see a model that reflects their age, size and race'.

Shulman was invited to give evidence at Jo Swinson's inquiry but turned her down. 'I'm very anti-legislation, anti-government initiatives. I don't think they need to get involved. God knows they've got enough to be thinking about without worrying about sample sizes. And it isn't just about "common sense".'

I'm learning this. I ask her about other myths – are there any commonly held beliefs about *Vogue*, the industry and body image? Her eyes fall on the magazine shelf. 'Ah! I know one!' she says, leaning in. 'We shot Adele for our October cover, and everyone said: 'How typical of *Vogue* – they shoot Adele and only show a head shot.'' It's true – bloggers were disgusted that they hid her size-16 body.

'But Adele would not let us pull the camera back,' Shulman explains. 'As soon as any of her body was shown on the camera's digital screen she'd say no. It was her desire to have a head shot, which I found very frustrating. I was desperate for a full-length picture.' That issue was one of the worst-selling in *Vogue*'s history.

I remember Orbach explaining that none of us lives in a vacuum. '*Vogue*,' Shulman continues, 'is one of very few [women's interest] magazines that never publishes diets, never points out when someone's put on weight. We don't come from that unhelpful culture where you forensically examine the way a woman looks. That's appalling. We don't have to put our hands up about that.'

Are today's diets – the way we are encouraged to eat cognitively – to blame for our anxiety? An eating-disorder specialist at the inquiry confirmed that the 'Atkins diet generates many cases for my work', but the problem is not eating disorders but disordered eating. Disordered eating includes competitive dieting and eating in secret – it can lead to both eating disorders and obesity, but more commonly just adds to the eater's anxiety.

Rates of depression in women and girls doubled between 2000 and 2010; the more women self-objectify, the more likely they are to be depressed. Could the mainstream media's warm embrace of disordered eating have contributed to that rise? *Grazia* reports that Beyoncé lost 60 lb of 'baby weight' by eating only lettuce. *Cosmopolitan* wrote about Kate Middleton's 'Dukan diet', which begins with seven days of pure protein, and later two 'celebration meals' a week. If women don't look like Beyoncé or Kate Middleton, their flat stomachs a testament to their stamina, then, it seems, they are not working hard enough.

One celebrity whose body is frequently scrutinised (and scorned)

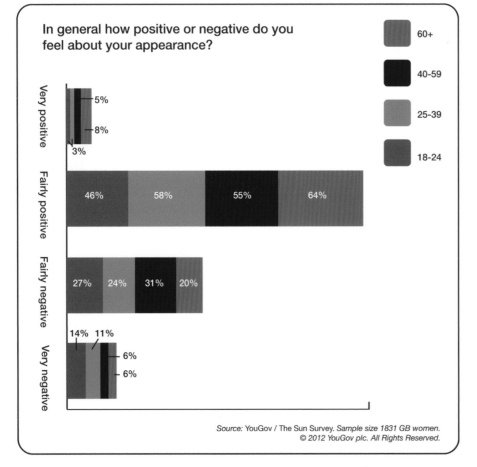

In general how positive or negative do you feel about your appearance?

60+
40-59
25-39
18-24

Very positive: 5%, 8%, 3%

Fairly positive: 46%, 58%, 55%, 64%

Fairly negative: 27%, 24%, 31%, 20%

Very negative: 14%, 11%, 6%, 6%

Source: YouGov / The Sun Survey. Sample size 1831 GB women.
© 2012 YouGov plc. All Rights Reserved.

by the tabloid media is *The Only Way is Essex*'s reality star Lauren Goodger. 'Never heard of Spanx, Lauren? Miss Goodger shows off muffin top in very unflattering dress,"'read one *Mail Online* headline. There are 546. 'Oops, maybe you should've tried the next size up. Lauren Goodger's tiny dress feels the strain.' 'Haven't you learned your lesson? Lauren Goodger steps out in ANOTHER pair of unflattering leggings.' Rather than the corrosive dripping-tap effect of reading these once a day over the last two years, read together these 546 headlines feel like quiet waterboarding.

I meet Goodger at Max Clifford's office. She is weeks into a 'drastic diet plan'. Many women feel judged on their appearance in some way, but what does it feel like to have those verdicts read by 99 million people a month? 'It is quite… draining,' she says. 'I can't look at comments. I can't buy the mags any more. I used to love them, but I was happy then. Then my weight became a story, not just for the show but for the press. Yeah, I'm definitely aware of the online scrutiny. My body becomes my work.' She thinks for a bit. 'But just because someone's not a size ten it doesn't mean she's a bad person.'

Last year Goodger had a nose job because, she said, she'd hated seeing her profile on TV. Most of her female *TOWIE* cast members have had cosmetic surgery – mainly breast implants, a bum lift, Botox, lip fillers. 'Where does it come from, the idea that natural is not beautiful, that we all need the model look?' Goodger asks herself. In response to Jo Swinson's inquiry, the British Association of Aesthetic Plastic Surgeons (BAAPS) has called for a ban on adverts for cosmetic surgery, highlighting promotions that play on vulnerabilities, such as 'divorce feel good' packages of breast augmentation and liposuction, and surgical procedures sold via online discount sites such as Groupon.

'Do you think there should be psychological screening for those seeking surgery?' I ask Goodger tentatively. 'It's a subject that's hard to talk about,' she says. 'Especially because I'm… within it.'

We talk about the idea of 'naughty' food, about the different expectations for men and women, about the celebrities who say they're 'big and happy' then suddenly lose weight. There's a pause.

'My little sister was anorexic at 11,' she says suddenly. "It started with someone at school calling her Miss Piggy. I mean, I didn't even know about dieting until I was 18. Things have changed so much. She gets the mags, she wants the bags, the Prada shoes. It's crazy. She's a baby! She wears lashes, make-up. But you do what everyone else is doing – you compare yourself. She's fine now, a year and a half later. But she'll message me going: "Have you lost weight? You look really good" and I'll think: God, don't say that.'

Goodger and I were both born in the 80s. In our lifetime (one that has seen the Internet enter our homes, along with hundreds more television channels), expectations of beauty have changed enormously. What must it be like growing up today, when cosmetic surgery is advertised on public transport, when 'baby-weight loss' diets are rife?

I gather together a group of under-20-year-olds at Livity, Brixton's 'youth engagement agency', to talk about body image. It's not a concept that needs explaining to them. Apart from Stephen (who says: 'The fact that I don't have an opinion on body image probably says something itself. Boys have it easier, definitely'), they have much to say.

First, some fictions they are keen to shatter. The pressure, the girls agree, is not, in fact, to be skinny – instead it's to look sexy. 'Hot.' 'Everyone wants to look like Kim Kardashian, even though we know she's a boring person – we don't want to have her personality, just her body,' says Claudia. 'Not Kate Moss's. Curves, not bones.'

This is the first time sex has been discussed – until now, everybody has talked about thinness and control, rather than changing your body to attract a boy. But as Bridget points out, you can starve yourself bony: 'The sexy body is much more unattainable.' 'I think our generation

is really savvy about the media,' says Amber as they move quickly on to the subject of airbrushed ads. 'So you know an image has been manipulated, but I suppose… you don't know what that's doing to you.'

I wonder about the fact that these young people are so literate in the issues of body image (as opposed to simply 'bodies') that their thoughts on the subject are so close to the surface. 'We're forced to think about it!' says Bridget. 'It's on every channel, every night. Programmes like *Supersize vs Superskinny*, or *How to Look Good Naked*, or freaky ones like *Half Ton Mum*, or *A Year to Save My Life*.' Everyone shouts out names – programmes about overhauling your body with diets, clothes or surgery. 'They have mixed messages,' says Amber. 'On one hand they're saying "love your body", then on the other "fat's bad, the worst thing you could do is be obese". The message "be healthy and do exercise" is a bit different from "be happy in your skin", isn't it?' The rhetoric of empowerment, here, actually disempowers.

Do we hate our bodies because of reality makeover TV? Susie Orbach describes how they often provide 'dysmorphic and distressed women' the opportunity to 'compete over their body distress and win the prize of radical restructuring'. The earliest technologies of body enhancement utilised techniques used on Second World War burn victims. 'To hear [winning reality show contestants] tell it,' Orbach says, 'they've been through their own individual wars, too… Their compulsion to change their bodies is a result of a different kind of assault on women, and increasingly men, which is sufficiently damaging to have persuaded them that the bodies they live in are urgently in need of transformation.'

Both the cosmetic surgery and the cosmeceutical industries (anti-ageing products) are growing, fast. It's these industries, 'along with the fashion houses, the diet companies, the food conglomerates [which own the diet companies], the exercise and fitness industry, and the pharmaceutical and cosmetic surgery industries', that Orbach is now combating, because, she says, 'they combine, perhaps inadvertently, to create a climate in which girls and women come to feel that their bodies are not OK'.

'Women stand in the ladies' loos complaining about their boobs or comparing their limbs to their colleagues'

Orbach debated with representatives from the diet industry in Parliament to applause from the public gallery – outside women protested with placards saying: 'Riot, don't diet.' Discussing Weight Watchers' recent £15 million TV ad, she suggested it was affordable to them only because their members are locked into lifelong 'straitjackets' of unrealistic weight-loss expectations. When I speak to her later, she goes further. 'I do think we should be prosecuting the diet industry for false advertising,' she says firmly. If dieting worked, she argues, you'd only have to do it once. There is evidence that diets may in fact contribute to fat storage and that, in giving a sense that food is 'dangerous', create conditions for rebellion, which eventually makes people fatter than they were to start with.

When I began my research, all roads led back to Orbach. She's been crucial in hammering home the dangers of body-image anxiety, yet figures show that we are feeling worse about our bodies than ever. 'You have to make the argument that this isn't trivial, then you have to make the argument that this is a substantial issue, then you have to combat the industries. I'm exhausted by it,' she says, throwing her head back. 'But what other options do we have?'

She's working on a psychoanalytic research project on the transmission of body image from mothers to daughters, and she's pushing for interventions by midwives, trained to show new mothers how their own body-image dissatisfaction will affect their babies. 'New mums are caught up in problems with their own bodies when they're bringing a new body into the world. We need a counterpoint to the nonsense that you should have a pre-pregnancy body six weeks after having a baby, or ever. What's the erasure about? That's where it should start.' She takes a breath. 'And teachers – it's all very well them taking classes about body image, but if they don't raise their own awareness about their own distress, then they're just passing it on.'

Back at the Centre for Appearance Research, we make our way down the narrow university corridors for lunch. In this surprise heat, the café is full of academics fanning themselves with menus, the odd bare-legged man. I am feeling a bit hopeless. All the statistics about sadness; all the people, like me, who aren't able to enjoy their own health, privilege, relative youth, because of this niggle. This feeling that we don't look right.

Jo Swinson's report detailed various recommendations being put to government, regulators, voluntary organisations and the private sector. In light of Orbach's evidence, they call for a review of the 'inaccurate' body mass index as the standard way of determining whether somebody is overweight, and for better support for new mothers. They ask advertisers to reflect 'consumer desire for authenticity and diversity', and for tougher regulation of the cosmetic surgery industry. But all the people I interviewed balanced their delight at the inquiry with a healthy wodge of cynicism at how much change these recommendations would effect.

And I wonder what we can do – us lot, the people with the faces we don't like, with the cankles, the muffin tops, the limp, lifeless hair. It's in the personal, day-to-day things, I think. Like consuming media critically. The media is a construction – this is no secret. Magazines, film, TV, newspapers – they all rely on advertising. So reminding ourselves that the body types we see represented are the body types that generate purchases. Asking ourselves: 'Am I being sold something here?' It's not a terrible thing, being sold to, it's just a... thing. Unpicking the media we consume, and talking about it, will help us feel better eventually. Cognitive dissonance programmes in schools have been effective – encouraging young people to speak out against the unrealistic ideals of beauty they see. In talking about it we reduce the internalisation of beauty ideals, and feel less awful about our implied failings.

I tell CAR's Dr Phillippa Diedrichs about something Amber mentioned – about femininity and dieting.

'Eating becomes a means of communication,' Diedrichs says after lunch. 'In our food choices we're demonstrating our femininity.' But it goes further than that. 'We're socialised to be negative about our bodies,' she says, and a slideshow of moments flashes through my head. Women standing in the ladies' loos complaining about their boobs. Or comparing their limbs to their colleagues' unfavourably. She introduces me to the idea of 'fat talk', everyday conversation that reinforces the 'thin ideal' and contributes to our dissatisfaction. Like: 'You look great – have you lost weight?' Or, on being offered a bun: 'Ooh, I really shouldn't.' 'After three minutes of fat talk,' says Diedrichs, 'there's evidence that our body dissatisfaction increases significantly.' Naming this – fat talk – makes much sense to me.

After a day at CAR, my body-image anxiety hasn't disappeared, but I can at least see a way to control it. We hate how we look because of our new, complicated visual culture, because of a fashion industry that has not adapted, a media that forensically analyses women's bodies and saturates our culture with body-change stories. Because of the rise of cognitive eating, the increasing abilities and accessibility of cosmetic surgery. Because to be feminine, today, means to hate your body.

I leave their building feeling quite different from when I arrived. I have the same legs, the same face, the same teeth, but something in my mind has changed.

10 June 2012

⇨ The above article originally appeared in the *Guardian* and is reprinted with permission. Please visit www.guardian.co.uk for more information.

Disturbing trend as schoolkids post videos asking strangers: 'Am I ugly?'

A disturbing trend for young girls and boys to post videos of themselves asking 'Am I Ugly?' is sweeping the Internet.

By Keith Kendrick

In the YouTube videos, 11, 12, 13 and 14-year-olds reveal their anxieties about their looks and ask viewers for reassurance.

But instead of being comforted, the youngsters are attacked by notoriously cruel online commentators.

The worrying trend has mushroomed of late, though the videos first started appearing two to three years ago.

One video, uploaded by sgal901, sees a pretty young blonde asking whether she is ugly and posing in a selection of photographs.

Her film has been watched more than 3,505,000 times since being uploaded in December 2010.

The comments that follow are either over-the-top compliments, suggesting sex, or painfully cruel.

One watcher wrote: 'This is such a stupid video...What stupid person would record a video like this one and then upload on YouTube don't they notice that they are just embarrassing their self by the way you are ugly the only thing I see in this video is ugliness I see no beauty.'

Others are kinder.

One wrote: 'Ignore those who comment "ugly". My opinion; You're super pretty.'

There are scores of other similar videos, their subjects wide-eyed and naïve.

Beautifulandproud posted a clip on 2 December 2011. She seems distraught and the video is heartbreakingly sad. She asks the question simply and gives no background or details.

'A lot of people tell me I'm ugly. I think I'm ugly and fat.' She says.

Faye, going by the YouTube name of Smilelovebeauty8, explains that at school she is often told she is ugly, but her friends tell she her she is pretty, so she asks YouTube viewers to tell her what they think.

The replies are abusive and crude.

But while the majority of videos are made by girls, they are not alone. Boys are asking the same question and comments are just as vicious and snide.

Parentdish editor Tamsin Kelly said: 'It's so sad to see young people so insecure about their looks and so naïvely displaying their anxieties to total strangers. It's an alarming step up from teen girls posting Facebook pics of themselves posing in new outfits or make-up and looking for compliments from their friends.

> **'Comments are either over-the-top compliments, suggesting sex, or painfully cruel'**

'As parents we strive to bring our children up to be happy and confident in their skins and if they are unhappy with their looks to come to their family and friends for reassurance. That's what makes these videos so heart-breaking – that these sad teens are turning to the Internet and anonymous eyes rather than real support.'

22 February 2012

⇨ The above information is reprinted with kind permission from Parentdish. Visit www.parentdish.co.uk for further information on this and other subjects.

Body image inquiry

The following comments are based on a consultation with young people from our Very Important Kids (VIK) group, who are aged between 12 and 24.

Who or what do you think is primarily responsible for influencing an individual's body image?

Parents can have either a positive or a negative influence on children and young people. The young people from our VIK group thought that this was particularly the case for young people up until their mid-teens, and when the young person was living in the family home. As the young person gets older, their peer group has more influence.

There are also external influences such as the media and fashion. A concern with these role models is that models are generally skinny, and 'perfect'. The message that this gives to young people is that you have to be skinny if you want to be successful, popular, etc. Famous people who have a weight problem, or are less than 'perfect', e.g. have cellulite, spare tyre, etc. are humiliated by the media. They have been known to print the most unflattering photographs, and highlight the cellulite, etc. Any famous people, who have a weight problem, are made a joke of by the media.

Are any particular groups particularly affected by poor body image? (e.g. socio-economic status, age, gender, ethnicity)? If so why?

Young people are particularly affected by poor body image. This is in part likely to be connected to their developmental age, but also the fact that they are bombarded with pictures in the media showing them what a 'perfect' body image should be.

There are issues for both males and females. It is well known that females have issues with body image, but there are also pressures on men as well to look a particular way. For instance, there are pressures put on men to be either a body builder, or a skinny rocker. Both of which are extreme body types.

Your body image is a reflection of your mental state, regardless of whether you eat too much or too little. Your body image isn't static, but can change depending on your circumstances and the context. It is connected to your lifestyle, and there is a correlation between body image and mental health. For instance, some medications can affect your weight, and conditions such as depression can prevent you from wanting to go out and partake in exercise. There are of course other mental health issues such as eating disorders, and body dysmorphic disorder, where people have a distorted body image.

> ### 'Your body image is a reflection of your mental state, regardless of whether you eat too much or too little'

Most young people are likely to be affected by issues associated with body image. However, young people with existing mental health issues will probably find it harder to cope with issues concerning body image.

At what age do you believe a person becomes aware of the need to reach appearance ideals?

Again this will depend on their background, but many will be aware of body image by primary school age.

What do you think has a positive influence on an individual's body image?

There should be lessons on body image in schools. This should be coupled with lessons on being healthy, e.g. body health, healthy diet, exercise and so o

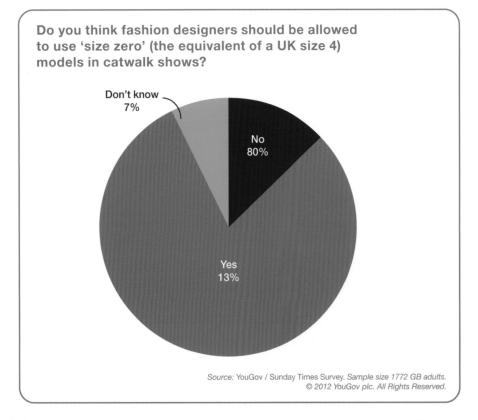

Do you think fashion designers should be allowed to use 'size zero' (the equivalent of a UK size 4) models in catwalk shows?

- No 80%
- Yes 13%
- Don't know 7%

Source: YouGov / Sunday Times Survey. Sample size 1772 GB adults.
© 2012 YouGov plc. All Rights Reserved.

The media and fashion industry could be a positive influence, but these companies would need to change their attitudes connected to using skinny models. There are some good examples, but they are in the minority.

What do you think has a negative influence on an individual's body image?

The media and the fashion industry can make people more anxious about their body image, and more paranoid about the way they look.

Young people face a lot of pressure concerning their body image. If these pressures make people more anxious etc. about their body image, then the stress may come out in different ways.

What are the links, if any, between obesity, eating disorders and poor body image?

People with eating disorders often have a distorted body image, and can believe that they are fat, even when they are dangerously thin. Eating disorders are also associated with stressful factors in their lives, and restricting their food intake gives them back some control over their lives.

'If you have a normal body weight, but want to be thinner, then being on a diet might help you achieve your "ideal" body image, but it could be dangerous'

In what way do you think body image anxiety affects a person's health and well-being?

Body image anxiety is likely to have a greater impact on young people with existing mental health problems. Having a negative body image is likely to result in people saying that it is impacting on their sense of well-being. The Good Childhood Inquiry found that ten to 15% of young people reported that they were unhappy with their appearance (Children's Society, 2012).

What are the economic, social and environmental costs to society from poor body image?

Poor body image can be a motivating factor to change something about your body that you don't like, such as being a bit overweight. However, this can be a serious problem when you dislike your body to the extent that you stop eating, over exercise, etc. in an attempt to change your body image.

Poor body image can often be associated with mental health and emotional well-being problems. There are about one in ten children and young people with a mental disorder (Green, 2005), and about 1.6 million people in the UK are affected by eating disorders (Beat, 2004). More than half of all adults with mental health problems were diagnosed in childhood. Less than half were treated appropriately at the time (Kim-Cohen, 2003).

Is there a deliberate strategy by some companies (e.g. in the diet, health, fashion and beauty industries) to generate poor body image in order to create a demand for goods and services?

The media bombards people with images about what they should be wearing, the make-up they need to be using and so on, and this can produce poor body image. The fashion industry uses unrealistically skinny models and this gives people, especially young people, an unrealistic idea of body image. These unrealistic ideas about how we should look, puts excessive pressure on young people to try and look a certain way. This can contribute to them developing eating disorders in an attempt to become skinny.

What steps, if any, do you think the following sectors can take to promote body confidence or address body image anxiety?

⇨ Advertising – use normal-sized people as well and don't just use skinny models. Therefore giving a more normalised view of body size/image. The way that women are portrayed needs to change. It isn't always seen as sexy to have a womanly figure, but a pre-pubescent figure is seen as sexy.

⇨ Education/schools – lessons that build resilience and self-esteem. The aim being to ensure that children and young people have good emotional well-being and have a healthy body image. Also, have specific lessons connected to body image.

'Schools need to have a greater understanding of eating disorders, and be more supportive'

Also, schools need to have a greater understanding of eating disorders, and be more supportive. We hear anecdotally that high achieving schools do not acknowledge that young people, often girls, have eating disorders. Not providing adequate support only makes the problem worse, and further stigmatises mental health issues.

⇨ Government – actively encourage schools to have lessons that build emotional well-being, and develop a healthy body image. At the moment the focus is on behaviour management and academic achievement. Schools that don't see the importance of emotional well-being, often overlook it.

⇨ Fashion industry – use normal-sized people, and don't use skinny models.

To what extent does the Government's response to poor body image (e.g. promoting health behaviour) represent value for money given the amount of resource put in which may undermine good body image?

Promoting health behaviours needs to include promoting emotional well-being and self-esteem as well as the importance of positive body image, to ensure that young people are more resilient and able to cope with the various pressures put upon them. However, mental health and emotional well-being are generally not covered very well, if at all, in PSHE lessons.

'There is a link between body image and people's mental state. Your body image can be positive and can change depending on your circumstances or context'

There needs to be regular, high quality work to address poor body image to ensure that it stands any chance of reducing the influence from the media, etc.

'Young people are particularly affected by poor body image'

Is there any evidence that diets and dieting improve or damage an individual's body image?

There is a link between body image and people's mental state. Your body image can be positive and can change depending on your circumstances or context. Dieting can improve your own body image, but it isn't necessarily always positive and can be very unhealthy. For instance, if you are currently over weight, dieting could improve your body image. However, if you have a normal body weight, but want to be thinner, then being on a diet might help you achieve your

'ideal' body image, but it could be dangerous

Other comments

Our main points are that young people with existing mental health problems generally find it harder to cope with the pressures put on them concerning body image. Young people, especially young women in highly pressured environments often develop eating disorders. Schools could help to build a positive body image, develop self-esteem and build resilience as part of PSHE lessons.

Young people from our VIK group have suggested that it would be helpful if relevant organisations such as YoungMinds, Beat, and Body Gossip come together to discuss these issues and make recommendations.

Members of the VIK have also expressed an interest to meet with the Chair of the Body Image APPG, to discuss this issue.

References

⇨ Beat website (2004) – http://www.b-eat.co.uk/about-beat/media-centre/facts-andfigures/

⇨ Children's Society (2012) The Good Childhood Inquiry report 2012. London, Children's Society.

⇨ http://www.childrenssociety.org.uk/sites/default/files/tcs/good_childhood_report_2012_final_0.pdf

⇨ Green, H., McGinnity, A., Meltzer, H. et al. (2005). *Mental health of children and young people in Great Britain 2004*. London: Palgrave.

⇨ Kim-Cohen, J., Caspi, A., Moffitt, T.E. et al. (2003): Prior juvenile diagnoses in adults with mental disorder. *Archives of General Psychiatry*, vol 60, pp.709–717

⇨ The above information is reprinted with kind permission from YoungMinds. Visit www.youngminds.org.ukfor more.

© 2012 Young Minds

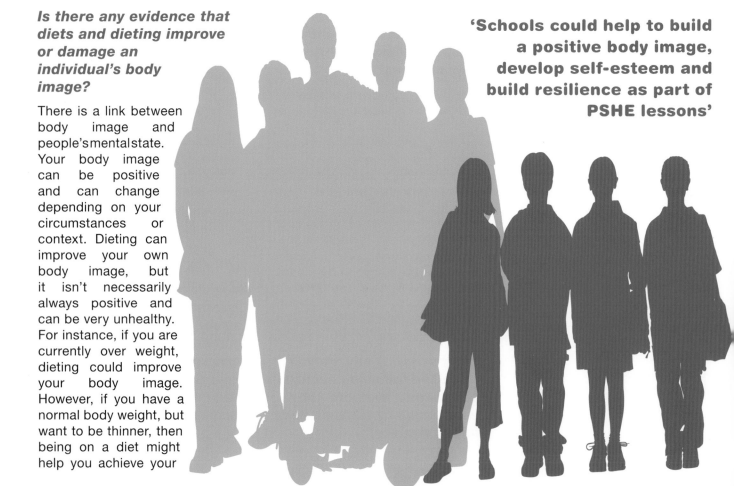

'Schools could help to build a positive body image, develop self-esteem and build resilience as part of PSHE lessons'

Body image concerns more men than women, research finds

Anxiety about body image has led to some men conceding they would exchange a year of their life for the perfect physique.

By Denis Campbell, health correspondent

More men worry about their body shape and appearance – beer bellies, 'man boobs' or going bald – than women do about how they look, according to research.

More than four in five men (80.7%) talk in ways that promote anxiety about their body image by referring to perceived flaws and imperfections, compared with 75% of women. Similarly, 38% of men would sacrifice at least a year of their life in exchange for a perfect body – again, a higher proportion than women.

'These findings tell us that men are concerned about body image, just like women. We knew that "body talk" affected women and young people and now we know that it affects men too,' said Dr Phillippa Diedrichs, from the Centre for Appearance Research at the University of the West of England. She conducted the study, of 394 British men, which was commissioned by Central YMCA and the Succeed Foundation, an eating disorders charity.

'men have high levels of anxiety about their bodies'

The survey revealed that men have high levels of anxiety about their bodies and that some resort to compulsive exercise, strict diets, laxatives or making themselves sick in an attempt to lose weight or achieve a more toned physique.

⇨ 80.7% talked about their own or others' appearance in ways that draw attention to weight, lack of hair or slim frame.

⇨ 30% have heard someone refer to their 'beer belly', 19% have been described as 'chubby' and 19% have overheard talk about their 'man boobs (moobs)'.

⇨ 23% said concerns about their appearance had deterred them from going to the gym.

⇨ 63% thought their arms or chests were not muscular enough.

⇨ 29% thought about their appearance at least five times a day.

⇨ 18% were on a high-protein diet to increase muscle mass, and 16% on a calorie-controlled diet to slim down.

Rosi Prescott, Central YMCA's chief executive, said: 'Historically, conversation about your body has been perceived as something women do, but it is clear from this research that men are also guilty of commenting on one another's bodies, and in many cases this is having a damaging effect.' Men's high levels of body talk were symptomatic of a growing obsession with appearance, she added.

Some three in five men (58.6%) said body talk affected them, usually negatively. Some 12% said they would trade a year of life if they could have their ideal body weight and shape, 15.2% would give up two to five years, 5.3% would forego six to ten years and 5.3% would sacrifice a decade or more.

Some 4% said they had made themselves sick to control their weight, while 3.4% reported using laxatives for the same purpose. Almost a third (31.9%) had "exercised in a driven or compulsive way" in pursuit of that goal, although that might have been partly due to 52% of the respondents being gym members, when the average is 12%.

Respondents, of whom about a quarter were gay men, blamed the media and celebrities for unhelpfully reinforcing unrealistic ideals of physical perfection. "Girls want to be slim and males want to be big and lean, and while it isn't a bad thing for people to want to look better, it has become more like a competition, which has a bad effect on most people's mental health,' said one respondent.

> **'There's been a big increase in the numbers of British men having cosmetic procedures such as a nose job or removal of breast tissue'**

Alan White, a professor of men's health at Leeds Metropolitan University, said: 'These findings are worrying but not surprising. There's been a big increase in the numbers of British men having cosmetic procedures such as a nose job or removal of breast tissue; that's gone from almost nothing to quite a significant industry over the last ten years. All this fuels the idea of the body beautiful and encourages a quick fix rather than appropriate diet and physical fitness levels.'

6 January 2012

⇨ The above article originally appeared in the *Guardian*. Visit www.guardian.co.uk for further information.

30% of women would trade at least one year of their life to achieve their ideal body weight and shape

Information from the Centre for Appearance Research (CAR).

Latest research conducted for new eating disorder charity The Succeed Foundation, in partnership with the University of the West of England (UWE), has found that 30% of women would trade at least one year of their life to achieve their ideal body weight and shape.

Dr Phillippa Diedrichs from the Centre for Appearance Research at the University of the West of England, said, 'The survey took place on university campuses around the UK. The findings highlight that body image is an issue for all women and not just adolescent girls as is often thought.

'The other really important finding is that the majority of women surveyed said that more needs to be done to promote positive body image on their university campuses.

'In response to this, this weekend the Succeed Foundation in collaboration with the Centre for Appearance Research at the University of the West of England, is launching "The Succeed Body Image Programme". The programme is based on over eight years of scientific research. This research has shown that similar programmes overseas are effective in reducing the onset of eating disorders and in promoting positive body image among women at university.

'The Succeed Body Image Programme is designed by experts, but will be run on university campuses throughout the UK by the students themselves. It's an extremely exciting programme that has amazing potential to improve the health of British women.'

The research has also found that in order to achieve their ideal body weight and shape:

⇨ 16% would trade one year of their life

⇨ 10% would trade two to five years of their life

⇨ 2% would trade six to ten years of their life

⇨ 1% would trade 21 years or more of their life.

The survey conducted at British Universities by Dr Diedrichs also discovered that in order to achieve their ideal body weight and shape, 26% of the women surveyed were willing to sacrifice at least one of the following:

⇨ £5,000 from their annual salary (13%)

⇨ A promotion at work (8%)

⇨ Achieving a first class honours degree (6%)

⇨ Spending time with their partner (9%)

⇨ Spending time with their family (7%)

⇨ Spending time with their friends (9%)

⇨ Their health (7%).

The survey results suggest that body dissatisfaction was common among the women surveyed, with one in two women saying that more needs to be done on their university campus to promote healthy body image.

⇨ 46% of the women surveyed have been ridiculed or bullied because of their appearance.

⇨ 39% of the women surveyed reported that if money wasn't a concern they would have cosmetic surgery to alter their appearance. Of the 39% who said they would have cosmetic surgery, 76% desired multiple surgical procedures. 5% of the women surveyed have already had cosmetic surgery to alter their appearance.

⇨ 79% of the women surveyed reported that they would like to lose weight, despite the fact that the majority of the women sampled (78.37%) were actually within the underweight or 'normal' weight ranges. Only 3% said that they would like to gain weight.

⇨ 93% of the women surveyed reported that they had had negative thoughts about their appearance during the past week. 31% had negative thoughts several times a day.

⇨ When asked which celebrity has the perfect body, Kelly Brook came top of the list.

Editor's notes

320 women studying at 20 British universities completed The Succeed Foundation Body Image Survey in March 2011.

Age Breakdown: Range 18–65 years. Average age=24.49 years.

In response to the fact that it is common for women attending universities to have body image issues, on 2 and 3 April 2011, The Succeed Foundation is launching The Succeed Body Image Programme in UK universities. This is a scientifically supported programme that aims to improve body image and prevent the onset of eating disorders.

The Succeed Foundation was founded in 2010 by Karine Berthou, with the mission of raising awareness and providing support for those affected by eating disorders. The aim is to introduce new programmes and fresh research to halve the average recovery time of sufferers; by creating networks, delivering programmes and adapting new technologies in prevention, education and coaching. All programmes or projects are scientifically supported and easily replicable, enabling availability to the widest number possible.

The Centre for Appearance Research (CAR) is a multi-disciplinary research centre based at the UWE, Bristol. CAR strives to make a real difference to the lives of the many hundreds of thousands of people with appearance-related concerns both in the United Kingdom and across the world. CAR acts as a focus and centre of excellence for psychological and interdisciplinary research in appearance, disfigurement, body image and related studies.

31 March 2011

⇨ The above information is reprinted with kind permission from the Centre for Appearance Research at the University of the West of England. Visit www.uwe.ac.uk for further information on this and other subjects.

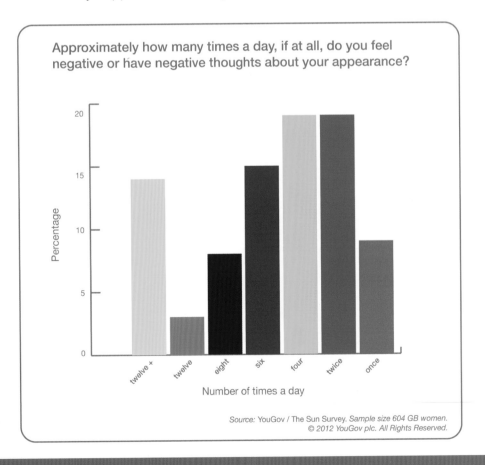

Approximately how many times a day, if at all, do you feel negative or have negative thoughts about your appearance?

Percentage (y-axis) / Number of times a day (x-axis): twelve +, twelve, eight, six, four, twice, once

Beer belly is biggest body issue for men

Information from the Centre for Appearance Research (CAR).

New research shows that men have serious issues and that talking about your body is no longer confined to women.

A major national study[i] examining British men's attitudes to their appearance reveals that over four in five (80.7%) men regularly engage in conversation about one another's body and that most are unhappy with their muscularity. The study found that men talk most about their unhappiness with their stomach, referred to most commonly as their beer belly.

'Over half of men questioned (58.6%) said that body talk affects them personally, mostly in a negative way'

The study, a collaboration between experts at the Centre for Appearance Research (CAR) at UWE Bristol, the Succeed Foundation and Central YMCA, also revealed that more than 35% of men would sacrifice a year of life to achieve their ideal body weight or shape. The majority of men surveyed were unhappy with their level of muscularity – most didn't think their arms (62.8%) or chests (62.9%) were muscular enough.

Over half of men questioned (58.6%) said that body talk affects them personally, mostly in a negative way. This mirrors research in women which shows that listening to just five minutes of body talk can lower overall body confidence. Men revealed that body talk affected their self-esteem, made them more self-conscious and in some cases

prevented them from going to the gym.

Nearly all men questioned (95.5%) said they see or hear body talk in the media and that nearly four in five (80.7%) gym members admitted to engaging in body talk in the gym. The most popular terms men use to describe another man's appearance include commenting on his beer belly (74.5%); six pack (69.8%); or man boobs (moobs) (63%). Nearly half of men also used the terms 'chubby' (46.1%) and 'ripped' (42.4%) to describe another man's appearance.

'Body talk' is the term used to describe conversation in which men reinforce and buy into the unrealistic male body image 'beauty ideal' which emphasises leanness and muscularity, for example, by commenting on, and comparing their appearance to, this 'ideal'.

This desire for more muscle mass may explain why one in five (18.2%) men questioned is on a high protein diet, and nearly one in three (32%) use protein supplements.

Dr Phillippa Diedrichs, who conducted the study at the Centre for Appearance Research at UWE Bristol, said, 'This research really demonstrates that body image is an issue for everyone, and that we need to take a collaborative approach towards promoting an environment that values diversity in appearance and promotes healthy body image.'

Rosi Prescott, Chief Executive of Central YMCA which commissioned the research in partnership with The Succeed Foundation said, 'Historically conversation about your body has been perceived as something women do, but it is clear from this research that men are also guilty of commenting on one another's bodies; and in many cases this is having a damaging effect. The high levels of body talk that we have found in men are symptomatic of a growing

obsession with appearance. The fact that one in three men would sacrifice a year of life to achieve their ideal weight and shape is a worrying sign and suggests that men are placing more value on their appearance than on other things, including life itself.'

'This desire for more muscle mass may explain why one in five men questioned is on a high protein diet, and nearly one in three use protein supplements'

Karine Berthou, founder of UK-based eating disorders charity The Succeed Foundation, who co-commissioned the survey, said, 'Negative body image is a serious issue in our society and is a key risk factor in the development of eating disorders. 17.4% of men had a definite fear that they might gain weight every day and 31.9% of men reported that they had "exercised in a driven or compulsive way" as a means of controlling weight. This sort of disordered eating and exercise behaviour is deeply concerning and highlights that men must be included in eating disorder and body image programmes. Succeed is committed to providing such programmes for everyone.'

Editor's notes

Research was conducted by the Centre for Appearance Research – 384 British men took part in an online survey (Nov–Dec 2011).

⇨ The Centre for Appearance Research (CAR) is a multi-disciplinary research centre based at UWE Bristol. CAR acts as a focus and centre of excellence for psychological and interdisciplinary research in appearance, disfigurement, body image and related studies. http://hls.uwe.ac.uk/research/car.aspx

⇨ Central YMCA is a leading health and education charity and is working with young people in schools to raise

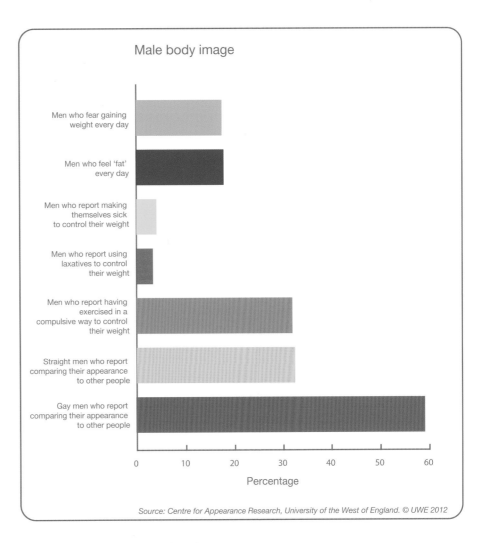

Male body image

Source: Centre for Appearance Research, University of the West of England. © UWE 2012

awareness of body image issues and is part of the Government's Expert Working Group on Body Image.

Central YMCA provides the secretariat to the All Party Parliamentary Group on Body Image which is currently conducting an inquiry into the causes and consequences of body image anxiety.

Further information on the group can be accessed here: www.ymca.co.uk/bodyconfidence/parliament

⇨ The Succeed Foundation is committed to supporting and developing innovative and evidence-based programmes and strategies to prevent and treat eating disorders and promote well-being. Founded in 2010 by Karine Berthou, The Foundation is focused on making available these strategies to men, women and children; young and old.

Together with individuals, carers, clinicians and researchers, The Succeed Foundation uses a holistic

approach to work towards creating a world free from eating disorders.

⇨ The Succeed Foundation has a number of male case studies with body issues, for synopsis please call Natalie Lisbona on 07801 551 282 or contact The Succeed Foundation press office – 020 7052 9203 / press@succeed-foundation.org

⇨ For more information about the research please go to: www.ymca.co.uk/bodyconfidence/bodytalk

6 January 2012

⇨ The above information is reprinted with kind permission from the Centre for Appearance Research at the University of the West of England. Visit www.uwe.ac.uk for further information on this and other subjects.

© UWE 2012

I love me

... it's very easy to be unhappy with our bodies in today's world. The pressure is on to look a certain way and this comes from many different directions.

The body of public opinion: attitudes to body image in the UK

Celebrities, gossip magazines, advertisers, and the fashion and fitness industries – all stand accused of an over-reliance on promoting a body 'ideal' which is either unrealistic or unattainable for over 95% of the population. The adulation of certain body types can make many of us feel insecure with who we are and have some damaging consequences:

⇨ Undermining our self-esteem and confidence

⇨ Leading to bullying and social exclusion

⇨ Responsible for disordered eating habits:

　⇨ One in four of us are on a diet at any one time

　⇨ Eating disorders such as bulimia and anorexia are at an all time high

　⇨ Discouraging some from participating in activities which can be good for their health (e.g. sports and exercise) because they don't feel like they belong.

What do the public think?

Central YMCA and the Centre for Appearance Research at the University of the West of England recently conducted a survey of 810 young people and 759 adults across the UK to explore public attitudes surrounding body image-related issues. Our research had a particular focus on the impact of images in the media and advertising on body image, in addition to finding out what people think about the numerous quick fixes that are available to change people's bodies.

Our research indicates that at least one in four adults feel depressed about their bodies. Young people also have issues with their bodies – over half of the adolescent girls (54.1%) surveyed said that girls at their school have body image problems and about a quarter of boys (23.7%) think that boys have body image problems.

Due to the widespread use of airbrushing and a lack of diversity in the appearances of people represented in the media, it is virtually impossible for most of us to achieve or maintain the bodies that we see on TV and in magazines. Therefore it's not surprising that our research found that:

⇨ About a quarter of girls (25.4%) compare their bodies to people on TV and over one third (35.2%) would like to look like the models who appear in magazines.

⇨ Over a third of men (36.8%) and over half of women (50.4%) report that they compare their bodies to people on TV.

⇨ Almost half of men (42.4%) and 30% of women said they would like their bodies to look like the models who appear in magazines.

Body diversity

Our research suggests that the public has an appetite for more diverse body images in media and advertising.

Almost half of adults (48.9%) said they wanted to see different body shapes and sizes, varieties of ages, ethnicities and a wider range of physical appearances in the media, advertising and fashion industries and on TV.

The public feel that the media and advertisers are still heavily reliant on using ultra thin or highly muscular body types in advertising and marketing.

Airbrushing

⇨ Almost three quarters of adults (70.6% of men and 80.9% of women) think that consumers are not aware of the extent to which images of people in the media have been airbrushed.

⇨ Over half of men were surprised by the extent of airbrushing in images presented to them.

⇨ There is broad agreement from men and women that airbrushing.

What about quick fixes to body confidence?

We asked the public to what extent they would be prepared to adopt

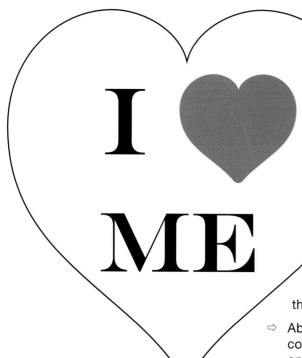

a quick fix solution to feel better about their bodies.

What do adults think about quick fixes?

⇨ Almost half of men (44.5%) and nearly three quarters of women (70.9%) have been on a diet in an attempt to change their body shape.

⇨ Nearly 10% of men (8.5%) would consider taking steroids to change their body shape.

⇨ Almost a third of men and women (28.2%, 31.4%) believe that cosmetic surgery is too readily available and should be restricted to those with underlying health issues.

⇨ Despite this, if money wasn't an issue a quarter of men (24%) and a third of women (29.5%)

would have cosmetic surgery to change their body shape.

What do young people think about quick fixes?

⇨ Roughly a third of adolescent boys (34.4%) and half of girls (49.1%) have been on a diet in an attempt to change their body shape or to lose weight.

⇨ A fifth of boys (17.7%) have taken protein supplements to make themselves more muscular.

⇨ Over one in ten boys (11.1%) would take steroids to build muscle if they were unhappy with the way they looked.

⇨ Nearly 10% of boys and girls (8.3% and 7.7%) would start taking laxatives to lose weight if they were unhappy with the way they looked.

⇨ Nearly 15% of girls would start taking diet pills to lose weight if they were unhappy with the way they looked.

The most desired cosmetic procedures among adolescents were:

⇨ Breast implants (14.7%)

⇨ Rhinoplasty (7.7% of boys a 11.5% of girls)

⇨ Botox (9.8% of girls).

⇨ The above information is reprinted with kind permission from Central YMCA. Please visit www.bodyimage.org.uk for further information.

© Central YMCA

Body image and mental health

Equality and life chances.

By Rupy Kaur, Disability Coordinator

In today's society we are constantly bombarded by images of perfection. Billboards and posters surround us everywhere of beautiful people – whether you are standing at the bus stop, with images of Cheryl Cole staring back at you, or walking into a newsagent to be confronted with copies of magazines such as *Glamour* and *Vogue*. It has been argued within the psychological and sociological world that these images have become our ideals and have therefore have affected the way we act and behave. Everybody wants to be perfect – even politicians are at it – we all know that David Cameron has been airbrushed in his latest poster campaign.

Research demonstrates that these images can lead to mental health issues such as, low self-esteem and depression due to us not being able to reach 'ultimate perfection'. Further mental health issues are becoming more common such as, anorexia and bulimia – John Prescott suffered

with bulimia for quite a while. Eating disorders are extremely detrimental to people's health – it was predicted that Brittany Murphy died from such a thing. Additionally, we all know that sunbeds can increase the chances of skin cancer, yet a majority of us still use them so that we can become one step closer to becoming perfect.

Negative body image is definitely a concern and people should be made aware of its impact, especially when it comes to young people. The Channel 4 presenter, Gok Wan, noted most famously by his hit TV series, *How To Look Good Naked,* campaigned heavily last year to try and get 'body confidence,' on the school curriculum as over 70% of teenagers are estimated to have little or no body confidence, leading to issues such as self-harm. This needs to stop and from a moralistic standpoint, I believe that we need to start acting and campaigning on such things.

The new series of *How To Look Good Naked* begins tonight at 8.00

on Channel 4. I am very excited about this as I believe that this show is much deeper than materialistic ideals. Wan challenges perceptions as he teaches people how to make the most of their body, by tackling self-esteem issues and ultimately increasing confidence. As a disabled activist, I am further excited, as his latest quest involves people with physical disabilities which is often overlooked in the fashion world. Wan tackles real issues to do with real people, and I think that we can all learn a lesson or two from him.

January 2010

⇨ The above information is reprinted with kind permission from Compass Youth. Please visit www.compassyouth.org for further information.

© 2012 Compass Youth

All Party Parliamentary Group inquiry on body image

Extract from the written evidence submitted by Lynne Featherstone, Minister for Equalities.

Opening statement

Thank you for inviting me to give evidence to the inquiry being undertaken by the All Party Parliamentary Group on Body Image. I am providing this evidence in my capacity as the Government's Minister for Equalities.

The Government recognises that low body confidence is a real issue in society, for men, women and children. We are firmly committed to this agenda and launched a Government body confidence campaign to address the problem.

The campaign has three aims:

⇨ We want to see a wider spectrum of healthy body shapes represented in popular culture, to include all ages and ethnicities, and different shapes and sizes. This is something that we need to work with industry to achieve.

⇨ We want to make sure people have a better understanding of the images they receive every day in the media. To do that, we must give individuals the tools to critically assess these images.

⇨ We want people to recognise that intellectual and emotional qualities – character and individuality – are equally expressive of beauty as narrow, physical appearance.

The Government's body confidence campaign has three main strands to achieve these aims:

⇨ We work with the media and other sectors to raise awareness of the issue of low body confidence and galvanise the debate on this important issue.

⇨ We work collaboratively with a range of industry bodies to tackle the causes of low body confidence.

⇨ We work with educational organisations to provide the tools people need to challenge images that can impact on their body confidence and self-esteem.

As Minister for Equalities I lead this work in government and work closely with ministerial colleagues in other departments to take this agenda forwards.

The Government is conducting a rapid evidence review to better understand the causes and consequences of negative body image, as well as identifying potential interventions. This analysis will look exclusively at the academic research on this topic. However, there is a variety of other research available, such as surveys and polling data, which informs this issue. Key findings from these include:

⇨ 57% of parents think that pictures in magazines and newspapers place too much pressure on children to conform to a particular body shape and size.[1]

⇨ 90% of teenage girls thought that statements about girls and women on TV and in magazines focus too much on what women look like, instead of what they achieve.[2]

⇨ 61% of young women think it is unacceptable for brands or products to use even minor airbrushing.[3]

⇨ 50% of women feel under pressure to look good at all times and 46% of women feel under pressure to lose weight.[4]

Questions from All Party Parliamentary Group on Body Image

From your perspective what do you think are the most damaging consequences of body image anxiety?

The impacts of body image anxiety can manifest in a variety of ways including: unhealthy eating behaviours (including eating disorders), low self-esteem (which can affect learning and careers, relationships and family, social life and hobbies), and depression. However, these impacts are the result of hugely complex and

1. TNS omnibus survey of parents, Bailey Review 2011

2. Girlguiding UK, Girls Attitudes Survey 2011

3. Credos, _Pretty as a Picture,_ 2011

varying factors and we must be extremely careful about attributing these consequences solely and specifically to body image anxiety.

'50% of women feel under pressure to look good at all times'

The Government is currently undertaking a rapid evidence review of the academic literature available on this topic. Once we have the results of this, we will have a clearer idea of what the most damaging consequences of body image anxiety are.

What do you see as effective approaches in promoting body confidence, and what evidence do you have that these approaches work?

Companies and industry organisations are hugely powerful in influencing popular culture and societal norms. They must be part of the solution, which is why we work closely with them. We have seen the Bailey Review of the commercialisation and sexualisation of childhood galvanise industry to take action to address parents' concerns, so we know it's possible when the will is there. However, education and building resilience is also crucial. Giving individuals the tools they need to really understand the images around them, and make them more media literate, can play a huge part in promoting body confidence. Once we have the results of the rapid evidence review on body image, we will be in a better position to understand what approaches work and where we can best target our intervention.

How can the Government encourage schools to provide an opportunity to learn about body image, either in the curriculum or as part of Personal, Social, Health and Economic Education?

Schools are already able to teach body image as part of PSHE education. The Government is currently conducting a review of PSHE education and body image will be considered as part of this review. The core curriculum does not require schools to include body image, but there is nothing to stop them incorporating the topic into core classes, such as physical education, if they think it is right for their pupils. Playing sport can contribute to children's health, well-being and confidence, and the Government wants to increase opportunities for young people to take part in sport. For example, the School Games is a new, four level school sport competition using the inspiration of the London 2012 Olympic and Paralympic Games to help transform sport in school and to get more young people playing sport.

What role should the Government, have on this issue, which Government departments do you think need to be involved and how might a co-ordinated approach be best achieved?

It is the Government's role to galvanise industry to take action, and support good practice wherever possible. The body image work has crossover with various other departments including the Department for Education, Department for Culture, Media and Sport, and the Department of Health. I regularly speak to ministerial colleagues in these departments, and this is also being taken forward by Home Office officials who liaise regularly with these departments.

What are the links between obesity, eating disorders and poor body image?

The Government is currently undertaking a rapid evidence review to ensure we are using the most robust and relevant evidence base to develop this policy area. Once we have seen the findings, we will be able to better understand the links between obesity, eating disorders and poor body image.

Do you believe that the level of regulation currently in place for goods and services which are marketed to enhance an individual's body confidence (for example, cosmetic surgery, supplements, diet programmes) is sufficient?

The Government is firmly committed to a voluntary approach to tackle the causes of low body confidence. Strict rules on the advertising of cosmetic surgery and other goods and services, overseen by the Advertising Standards Authority (ASA), are already in place. The advertising codes must be robust and based on best evidence. If new evidence emerged which clearly highlighted major problems in relation to consumer harm or protection of the vulnerable then we would expect the regulators to consider this fully and take appropriate action.

On 24 January 2012, the Government announced two reviews related to cosmetic surgery, one of which includes whether the regulation of the products used in cosmetic interventions is appropriate.

The terms of reference of this review explicitly ask it 'to consider... how to ensure that people considering [cosmetic] interventions are given the information, advice and time for reflection to make an informed choice'. We will be interested to read the findings of the reviews in relation to the Government's body confidence work.

26 April 2012

⇨ The above information is reprinted with kind permission from Central YMCA. Please visit www.bodyimage.org.uk for further information.

4. MORI Poll for International Women's Day 2012

Why responsible advertising to children should be top of the agenda

Unilever's chief marketing officer speaks to Jo Confino about the company's stance on responsible advertising, the power of social media to self-regulate and the reasons behind its banned Lynx advert.

By Jo Confino

'Talk to your daughter before the beauty industry does' is the tag line at the end of a short film from Unilever's Dove personal care brand showing how young girls are bombarded by advertising promoting a stereotypical vision of the perfect woman.

The film, *Onslaught*, is a powerful and disturbing illustration of how young women will go to any length to get the 'right look', ranging from bulimia to plastic surgery.

It also highlights the vulnerability of children to advertising and explains why a new set of Children's Rights and Business Principles, created by UNICEF, Save the Children and the United Nations Global Compact, urges business to use marketing and advertising responsibly.

The principles say companies need to recognise children's greater susceptibility to manipulation, and the effects of using unrealistic or sexualised body images and stereotypes.

Keith Weed, chief marketing officer at the multinational consumer goods company, is under no illusion that advertising has a powerful influence on the way we live our lives. He should know, given that Unilever is the second largest advertiser in the world.

'There was an argument in the 80s that advertising just moves consumption around. I don't believe that,' says Weed. 'We need to make sure that children are brought up in a way that respects and develops them. Advertising has a responsibility. We can create positive imagery but also can create negative imagery.'

Weed says the Dove campaign has had a tremendous impact in promoting a healthier vision of beauty and Unilever has banned the use of size zero models and ensures women used by the company's marketers and advertising agencies have a certain body mass index.

But isn't Unilever being hypocritical given that its advertising for Lynx deodorant, which is directed at teenage boys, promotes the very stereotypes of women that Dove seeks to challenge?

Only last November Lynx advertisements featuring glamour model Lucy Pinder were banned for degrading women and treating them as sex objects.

Pinder was seen wearing very little and flashing her cleavage in a series of provocative video advertisements.

The Advertising Standards Authority (ASA) ruled that the campaign was 'unsuitable to be seen by children and could cause them harm' and that the Rotten Tomatoes and Anorak websites, on which some of the films were placed, were not protected by age verification.

The ASA further ruled that the ads were 'likely to be seen as gratuitous and to objectify women' and that the tagline in two adverts to 'Play with Lucy' would 'also be seen as degrading to women. We therefore concluded that the ads were likely to cause serious and widespread offence.'

Weed says Lynx advertising is tongue in cheek and that it is aimed at a youth market: 'It's how an adolescent boy would love the world to be but that everyone, including them, knows it is not going to be.

'Occasionally we, like others, do not get every execution right. Since 1983 there have been millions of consumer impressions for Lynx and this is one incident and we responded accordingly.

'More than two billion people use our products every day and the last thing we want to do is alienate them. In fact mums are the biggest purchaser of Lynx so we are very careful they are not offended. If mums felt it was an inappropriate brand it would not go in their shopping baskets.'

Seven years ago Unilever voluntarily stopped all marketing communications directed primarily at children under the age of six years because it recognised that this age group does not have the cognitive ability to distinguish between advertising/marketing and programming.

Two years later this was extended to restrict marketing to children between the ages of six and 11 for all food and drink products except those that meet Unilever's nutrition criteria.

Unilever also bans the use of cartoon characters and celebrities on packaging, labelling and point-of-sale materials.

Weed says he is a great believer in self-regulation and points to the failed experiment in Sweden when restrictions on children's television advertising led to wall-to-wall American cartoons because there was no money to invest in local children's programming.

He also points out that the rise of social media means that parents have far more power to challenge inappropriate advertising directed at children.

'If social media can within three weeks bring down the Egyptian Government that has been in power for more than 30 years, just think what you can do to a consumer brand,' he says. 'Social media is giving people a voice and this will be the most effective method for ensuring that companies do not get out of hand, especially when it comes to the sexualisation of children.'

Unilever has been highlighted by UNICEF for showing best practice for its 'Dirt is Good' advertising campaign for Persil and Omo because of its success in 'creating awareness of children's right to play, the right to express themselves – in short, the right to be a child! It encourages parents to see the value of exploration, play, activity and exercise as critical to children's development and important for full and healthy lives, even if it means that children get dirty in the process.'

Weed says the Persil/Omo campaign is a classic example of a brand's ability to create positive behaviour change by showing every child has a right to experiential learning.

He also points to Unilever's work to establish hand washing and teeth brushing at an early age in developing country markets.

'The humble bar of soap is an amazing step in the right direction because proper hand washing reduces diarrhoea by 50%, which limits the number of deaths, leads to better school attendance and helps prevent stunting – one in four children are stunted either physically or mentally,' he says.

Unilever has made a commitment through its sustainable living plan to reach one billion people with its hand washing campaign by 2015, through a mixture of advertising, in-school education and NGO partnerships.

Its other campaigning is focussed around teeth brushing. Weed says that most behaviours are wired in as adults so the only way of building positive habits is when people are young.

'If we brush teeth twice a day, for example, it leads to 50% better oral hygiene, yet that does not happen for the vast majority of people globally,' says Weed. 'In fact there are more mobile phones in the world than toothbrushes. Our advertising shows fathers and their children having fun in the bathroom mucking around

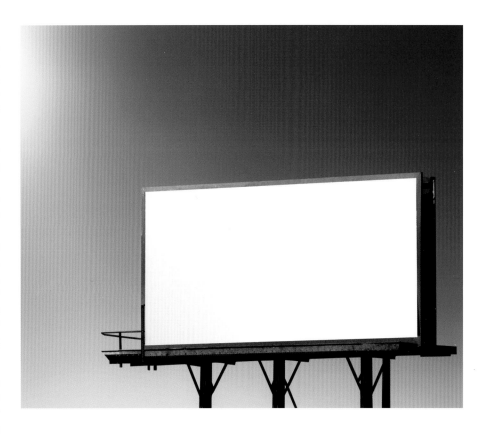

learning how to brush. By doing these campaigns we improve the behaviour around brushing.'

Given that Unilever operates around the world, Weed says it is important to have one set of rules that apply to all markets 'because a child is a child and has rights whatever culture you live in'.

However, he says there are pushbacks from individual countries that believe the rules around children are too restrictive.

Advertising also has to be culturally appropriate. For example, in China the Omo Dirt is Good advertisements had to be amended because the feedback from mothers was that experimenting with nature or playing with friends is considered frivolous and that children are expected to concentrate on their school work or learn to play a musical instrument.

Weed recognises the positive work that other companies are doing such as Colgate-Palmolive in the field of oral hygiene and points to the recent John Lewis Christmas campaign as an example of positive role modelling by showing the value of giving.

When asked to name the worst type of advertising aimed at children, Weed is quick to criticise marketing that encourages children to pester their parents to spend money: 'That

must be the worst because it adds an economic stress into the family.'

Tell us your thoughts

Unilever says there is a clear distinction between its Dove self-esteem campaign, which challenges a one-dimensional view of women's' beauty, and Lynx's tongue-in-cheek stereotyping of adolescent and young men's sexual fantasies.

Do you agree with them or do you believe that Lynx advertising devalues the company's strategy to promote positive imagery and ensure that children are protected?

Is it fair to highlight the Lynx advertisements or should the company be applauded for its policies towards responsible advertising to children and the work it does in the developing world to encourage positive habits such as hand washing and teeth brushing?

19 March 2012

⇨ The above article originally appeared in the *Guardian*. Visit www.guardian.co.uk for further information.

'Pretty as a picture'

The truth about airbrushing and advertising, by advertising's think tank Credos.

Do young women understand the term 'airbrushing'?

It has been claimed that young women don't realise that images in adverts have been airbrushed. This has resulted in calls for a 'kite mark' to be placed on photographs which have been digitally enhanced, to alert consumers to the practice. However, our research shows that young women are already well aware of the widespread digital manipulation of everyday images

Some 84% of young women know what the term 'airbrushing' means. The number is high even among pre-teens: over half (58%) say they understand the term, with awareness rising to 97% amongst 16–21-year-olds.

'Information about airbrushing is reaching young women mainly via TV programmes, magazines, and school or college'

These high levels of understanding are also reflected in the fact that 40% of young adults have used, or asked someone else to use, airbrushing techniques to make a photo of themselves look more attractive. The focus group discussions suggest that such photos are probably those posted on Facebook. One 14-year-old girl describes how: 'If you want to put a picture on Facebook, everyone's going to edit it a bit, to make themselves look better.'

Moreover, the majority of young women (85%) are aware when looking at magazines or advertising that sometimes the images have been airbrushed. Again, this figure is high amongst pre-teens, with 63% agreeing that they are aware, rising to 98% amongst young adults.

Their information comes from a variety of sources as outlined below:

These figures vary considerably depending on the age of the respondent, and to a lesser extent by social grade. Younger girls aged 10–15 are more likely to have learnt about airbrushing from a parent or guardian (47%), whereas young adults are more likely to have gathered information from TV programmes (62%) or magazines (55%). Young women are also more likely to have been educated about airbrushing by a parent or guardian if they are from a C1C2 (38%) or DE (35%) background, compared with fewer than a third of AB young women (28%).

This suggests that information about airbrushing is reaching young women mainly via TV programmes, magazines, and school or college. Education at school seems to be a particularly effective way of educating young women about airbrushing. One 13-year-old girl describes how in her ICT class she has been 'finding out about all the airbrushing, and you see how they get the computer and they edit it for, like, their legs to be skinnier, cellulite to be removed, their boobs to look bigger'.

Which images do you women prefer?

Once we understood what young women thought of idealised images and digital manipulation in advertising, Credos wanted to discover which type of images they prefer in advertising aimed at them. To test their preferences, we showed 1,000 young women four different images of the same model. Credos commissioned its own photo shoot because we were unable to find an unretouched image of a young healthy-sized model. We chose our model, Bella, because she is at the upper end of the age group we were polling and she is an average UK dress size 10-12. The original image of Bella was then manipulated to different degrees:

1. Completely unchanged, so we refer to it here as 'natural'.

2. Lightly retouched, removing minor blemishes and evening out her skin tone.

3. Bella's body shape was altered, slimming her to a UK size eight.

4. Bella has been made to look extremely thin - we estimate a UK size four.

Our question: 'Which of the following images would you choose to appear in an advert for women, or girls, like you?'

The answer: The majority (76%) of young women prefer either natural (image 1), or lightly retouched (image 2), over the heavily airbrushed images (images 3 and 4).

Young women's perceptions of 'flawless' models in adverts

Despite the fact that young women are aware of airbrushing in advertising, some continue to aspire to look like the re-touched images they see. Although 42% disagree that seeing airbrushed models in adverts makes them want to look like those models, over a third (37%) of young women say that it does. This proportion is worryingly high among pre-teens: a third (33%) of girls aged 10–12 agree with this statement, but it peaks among mid-teenage girls. Some 45% of 16–17-year-olds agree, falling slightly to 42% once young women reach 18 years of age. This suggests that improved knowledge of airbrushing does not necessarily mitigate the negative impact these images can have on young women's body confidence.

Young women tell us that they respond more positively to natural images. We asked them whether they think it is acceptable for brands or products to use airbrushing to erase blemishes or spots on models in their adverts. Almost a third (30%) of young women believe this is very unacceptable, and a similar

number (31%) consider it slightly unacceptable. The figure is highest among those in their early teens: over three quarters (77%) of 13–15-year-olds say this is unacceptable – 34% say it's very unacceptable, while 33% say it's slightly unacceptable.

'My arms are too fat. Now my legs are too short. Have I got muffin tops? My hair won't backcomb properly'

'I don't really take much notice of it. I wouldn't sit there and go, "I've got to go and get that hairspray, I've got to go and get that mascara, 'cause I might end up looking like Cheryl Cole".' Girl, 13

Young women's attitudes towards thin models in adverts

We also asked our respondents whether they agree with the statement 'seeing adverts using thin models makes me want to diet/lose weight/feel more conscious of the way I look'. While over a third (35%) of young women disagree with this statement, almost half (47%) of young women agree. It varies considerably by age, with mid-teens again the most likely to agree:

There is a significant difference between social grades when it comes to the statement 'seeing adverts using thin models makes me want to diet/lose weight/feel more conscious of the way I look'. Over half (52%) of AB young women agree with this statement, compared

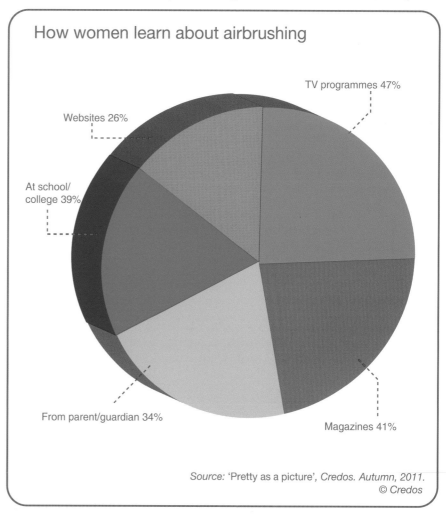

How women learn about airbrushing

TV programmes 47%
Websites 26%
At school/college 39%
From parent/guardian 34%
Magazines 41%

Source: 'Pretty as a picture', Credos. Autumn, 2011.
© Credos

with 40% of young women from a DE background. These differences are also reflected in the fact that almost two fifths (39%) of AB young women agree that they 'want to look like airbrushed models in adverts', compared with just under a third (32%) of DE young women.

Opinions are even more pronounced when it comes to airbrushing being used to change the body shape of a model in advertising. A large majority (84%) of young women believe that this is unacceptable, ranging from 78% of pre-teens to 89% of young adults. This shows that the older girls become, the less tolerant they are of this particular use of airbrushing.

'You see them in the mirror and her mood changes if she doesn't feel good in what she wears. She worries about what people think, a lot'

What the answers from both these questions suggest is that young women's body confidence is at its lowest when they leave compulsory education. This could be for two main reasons. First, 16 is the age at which young women reach the age of consent, and therefore concerns about their appearance are top of mind. Mums recognise this type of behaviour – one mother of a mid-teen describes how 'Getting ready to go out is stressful for her and me – every Friday she starts at about 4pm and goes on for about five hours until she goes out.'

Second, for those who enter a college or sixth form, it is the age at which many of them no longer have to wear a school uniform, and may therefore become more conscious of the way they look in comparison to their peers. They may also become more aware of their appearance because, rather than compare themselves to others in school uniform, they become part of the adult world – comparing themselves to older women who have more money to spend on fashion, hair and make-up.

'I don't really look at things like that and be like, "Oh, I wish I was that pretty"... I don't really sit there and like, cry and that, and be like, "Oh my God, why am I like this?" I just sometimes wish that I was that skinny and that tall.' Girl, 13

Mum's concerns

After speaking to the young women in our focus groups, we also spoke to their mums separately, producing some valuable insights into young women's lives.

Body image

The mum of a pre-teenage girl speaks for many when she says: 'Yes, it's a big one. Her hair, clothes, weight.' However, we also observed that their girls' preoccupation with the way they look is not always something that is spoken out loud. As one pre-teen's mum says, 'They don't

make it known – but you see them in the mirror and her mood changes if she doesn't feel good in what she wears. She worries about what people think, a lot.' Another says 'It's definitely a worry. My daughter put on weight, I could see that, and she talks about her body all the time – I think it's an obsession with her...' (mum of mid-teen).

'I don't really sit there and like, cry and that, and be like, "Oh my God, why am I like this?" I just sometimes wish that I was that skinny and that tall'

The girls' unspoken concerns tend to manifest themselves as 'tantrums' and self-critical behaviour. Mums list complaints such as 'I can't wear this. This looks wrong. My arms are too fat. Now my legs are too short. Have I got muffin tops? My hair won't backcomb properly' (Mum of early teen). The girls appear to worry a good deal about appearance – particularly their hair, but also spots and blemishes – usually for boys' benefit.

Autumn 2011

⇨ The above information is reprinted with kind permission from Credos. Please visit www.credos.org.uk for further information.

© Credos 2011

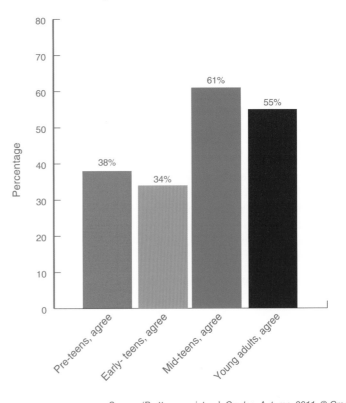

'Seeing adverts using thin models makes me want to diet/lose weight/feel more conscious of the way i look'

Source: 'Pretty as a picture', Credos. Autumn, 2011. © Credos

Health food magazine airbrush fattens up skinny model

One of the world's leading health brands, Holland & Barrett, has come under fire for altering the image of a model on its magazine cover to make her appear fuller-figured.

By Roya Nikkhah, Arts Correspondent

The retailer digitally modified, or 'retouched', the body shape of a model in an issue of *Healthy*, its customer magazine, to conceal her true thinness.

The revelation will fuel concerns about the 'size-zero' culture within the magazine industry, where increasingly-slender models are being used in photo shoots.

Details of the incident emerged during a round-table debate on the issue of retouching earlier this month, hosted by the model agency Leni's Model Management and attended by photographers, magazine editors and models including Jodie Kidd.

During the debate, Jane Druker, the editor of *Healthy* magazine – which promotes 'health and well-being' and has featured Elizabeth Hurley on its cover – admitted that Kamilla Wladyka, the model who features in the April issue, was so thin in real life that her image was radically retouched before appearing on the cover.

'We made her legs a little bit bigger, to make her look like she was a size ten as opposed to a size four'

Miss Druker told participants in the debate: 'She was so thin, we had to put on about half a stone.' Gerard Chevalier, a psychotherapist and former fashion photographer who also took part in the debate, said that Miss Druker went on to tell him the image had been enhanced to make the model appear two to three stone heavier than her actual weight. He said: 'She told me the girl was so thin, they had to put 15 to 20 kilogrammes on her.'

The *Sunday Telegraph* has previously revealed that fashion magazines are increasingly manipulating images of skinny models to make them look fuller-figured, in order to deflect criticism of promoting unhealthily-thin images.

But the use of such retouching in a health magazine will raise concerns that the magazine industry is simply ignoring the 'size-zero' issue. The details provided by Miss Wladyka's modelling agency clearly state that she is a very slender size six, with a 24-inch waist.

Susan Ringwood, the chief executive of the eating disorder charity, Beat, who has campaigned for magazines to use models of diverse sizes, described the use of the images as 'hugely disappointing'.

She said: 'There's a fundamental difference between using camera work to make someone look polished, and changing the shape and size of someone's body in order to portray them looking differently, to conform to whatever ideal.

'It's just not helpful and puts huge pressure on people to keep up a hyper-perfectionism that isn't real. If you can't trust the health industry to be healthy, how can you expect the fashion magazines to put their house in order?'

Eleni Renton, the director of Leni's Model Management, said that retouching photographs to make models appear larger was 'crazy'. She said: 'Rather than take a chance on a different size model who actually fits the criteria for a shoot, it's much easier for magazine editors and casting directors to book a girl who is a known quantity in the industry, even if she might be slightly too slim or large for a job, and then retouch her later.

'But when magazines start changing body shape, it becomes unhealthy. They are not acting responsibly. That girl probably should have been sent home from the shoot – she's supposed to be representing a "healthy" magazine as their cover girl and they retouched her to make her look healthier. It's false.'

'The model was so thin in real life that her image was radically retouched before appearing on the cover'

She also called for magazines to introduce a kite-mark system informing readers when images are modified: 'Retouching is getting increasingly out of hand. Most people can't tell how much is being used, so they are aspiring to unattainable fantasy images.

'Magazines should have signs indicating when an image has been retouched, so people can see at a glance how much work has been done.'

Miss Kidd said that retouching images to correct minor imperfections was acceptable, but condemned the practice of distorting models' body shapes. She said: 'Retouching for little blemishes is fine, but putting weight on, taking weight off, that goes too far.'

Miss Druker claimed that Miss Wladyka had appeared healthy during a casting for the photo shoot a week before it took place, but looked too thin to feature on the magazine's cover on the day of the shoot.

She said: 'Sometimes when you cast a model, they look OK, but then when they turn up on the shoot day, they might not have eaten for two or three days. You're not in charge of their health.

'There were plenty of clothes that we couldn't put on her because her bones stuck out too much'

'When she did arrive, there were plenty of clothes that we couldn't put on her because her bones stuck out too much. She looked beautiful in the face, but really thin and unwell.

'That's not a reflection of what we do in our magazine, which is about good health and women looking healthful and well.

'She was a stunningly beautiful girl and we knew what we were able to do with retouching. We made her legs a little bit bigger, to make her look like she was a size ten as opposed to a size four.

'It's not what we normally do and I would never want to mislead people.'

Holland & Barrett declined to comment.

15 May 2010

⇨ The above article originally appeared in *The Telegraph*. Visit www.telegraph.co.uk for further information.

© Telegraph Media Group Limited 2010

'Ban airbrushed photos aimed at teens,' says former anorexia sufferer Rachael Johnston

Eating disorder charity Beat has backed an anorexia sufferer's call to ban airbrushed photos of models in magazines.

Rachael Johnston, a 20-year-old former anorexia suffer, said she was obsessed with images of celebrities when she became ill at just 13.

Now Johnston, who plunged to just 4.5 stone during her illness has launched an e-petition with her mother Lynne which seeks to ban airbrushed images on adverts aimed at young children.

'I was cutting out pictures of models and celebrities and filling scrapbooks with them'

Susan Ringwood, chief executive of the eating disorder charity Beat said airbrushed images could be 'toxic' and harm the recovery of those with eating disorders.

'Everyone is influenced by images that do not portray reality. For those young people whose sense of self-worth is already low, this hyper-perfectionism is toxic.'

Ringwood, whose charity supports an All Party Parliamentary Group on body image added: 'We know the difference it would make to all young people's self-esteem and body confidence if they could be sure which of the images they see are natural and true to life.'

Johnston mentions in the e-petition how those under-16 are the 'most vulnerable to body image and body identity security'.

'By banning airbrushed images that target the under 16s, it would let the UK become the leading nation in giving the next generation positive and healthy messages through the media,' she writes.

She said how magazines and adverts affected her when she became ill, telling the *Daily Mail*: 'I was cutting out pictures of models and celebrities and filling scrapbooks with them. My obsession at the time was Victoria Beckham. I would cut out images of her body and stick my face on the top.

'I would write underneath, "This is what you have to be – she's perfect".'

'L'Oreal adverts featuring actress Rachel Weisz judged to be "misleadingly exaggerated" by the ASA'

The move follows Liberal Democrat MP Jo Swinson campaigning against heavily airbrushed images. In January, L'Oreal adverts for anti-wrinkle cream featuring actress Rachel Weisz were banned and judged to be 'misleadingly exaggerated' by the Advertising Standards Association following a complaint from Swinson.

30 April 2012

⇨ The above information is from *The Huffington Post*, reprinted with permission AOL (UK) Limited. Visit www. huffingtonpost.co.uk for further information.

© AOL (UK) Limited 2012

The debate: should body image lessons be introduced in schools?

In response to the* Reflections on Body Image *report, MPs have recommended that school children take part in compulsory body image and self-esteem lessons.

With girls as young as five now worrying about their appearance and cosmetic surgery rates increasing by nearly 20% since 2008, there are fears that young people have worrying and unrealistic perceptions of what is healthy.

But would introducing lessons act to affirm positive messages to young people? Or is body image a subject that simply can't be taught?

Nicky Clark supports the introduction of lessons, while Harriet Walker strongly disagrees. Which do you agree with?

For: Nicky Clark

The publishing of *Reflections on Body Image* makes for depressing statistical reading. It details, among other things, that the response to the three-month public inquiry co-ordinated by the APPG was that the ideal of physical perfection stems from 'media (43.5%), advertising (16.8%) and celebrity culture (12.5%) together account for almost three quarters of the influence on body image in society'.

'Every time I take my learning disabled daughter out of the house, she runs the gamut of looks, stares, verbal abuse and disdain'

The report explains that irrespective of how repeatedly we are 'told and sold' this image which we are conditioned to crave, 95% of the population will never achieve this.

I wholeheartedly welcome the idea of teaching body image classes to children because sadly we are at a point where we have to. This report

sourced experts and produced information and explanation which should make us all stop and question ourselves.

However sad it is to read the statistics which the report contains, there is a human cost of a societal view of the perfect body image bombarding us every day with an unreachable goal.

The net result of a pre-occupation with how we look is the fact that those who don't subscribe to the 'norm' suffer the wrath of those who do or those who try. What we are fast losing sight of is the notion that just because you look different doesn't mean you are incapable of feelings. This is best demonstrated by the sickening mocking response to the recent news of Georgia Davies, a 19-year-old in organ failure who collapsed from a seizure in her home. The fact that Georgia weighed 63 stone apparently negated any sympathy or recognition of her as a human being on the point of death. Her weight, we were assured, was her own and her family's fault, and therefore the wrath of her diversity was swift and vindictive. There was no wish to dig a little deeper and learn Georgia's story. Looking at her, it seems, was all the information some people needed to fuel their 'justifiable blame'.

We endure fear of difference too. Every time I take my learning disabled daughter out of the house, she runs the gamut of looks, stares, verbal abuse and disdain. She has learning disabilities, autism and epilepsy; she's also tall and draws the eye with her vocal sounds and physical gestures. She doesn't look like other people so she, like Georgia, mustn't feel the same things they feel. Both girls have been appraised in these perfection-dominated days of ours and found wanting.

I spoke to Susan Ringwood CEO of Beat, a national eating disorder charity which delivers training in schools in an effort to promote positive body image, who said:

'Body image isn't a trivial matter of just wanting to look good, it's a fundamental part of our identity. In its most serious form, we know that some people are particularly vulnerable to developing an eating disorder because their body image is so negative and distorted. That is why Beat is committed to providing secondary schools with lessons that can be part of building a positive body image. We know that will help everyone become more resilient to the influences that are positively toxic to some.'

Wallis Simpson, Duchess of Windsor once said 'you can never be too rich or too thin'. Sadly our children seem to be in desperate need of learning that in a diverse society these words are not an aspiration for life.

Against: Harriet Walker

The Government's proposal of body image classes for school children is a classic instance of those in power totally missing the point. That the *Reflections on Body Image* report was commissioned and – what's more – properly seen through, is a step in the right direction, of course, but this cod-science conclusion utterly nullifies the validity of its findings. It's yet another instance of buzzword-ism and watered-down social sciences purporting to be practical and useful in the quotidian.

But if body image classes come to pass, they'll be even more of an opportunity for dossing than career talks and PHSE.

Because body image is not something you can teach. It's something absorbed, from parents and friends, from culture and the media: these are those that need classes, not the innocent sponge that quietly sucks up whatever glossy, pouting imagery they are presented with from an early age. You can tell someone they're not fat, or that they're beautiful in their own way, until you're blue in the face, but they won't believe it until they see some form of public representation that they can identify with.

The problem lies not, as many would wag the finger and bluster about, with the fashion industry or the catwalk. Time was, models and high-end visuals were ubiquitous and influential on street culture, but the Internet and the rise of celebrity mean these sectors are no longer the last word in aspirational chic.

The study found that numbers of people choosing to have cosmetic surgery have gone up nearly 20 per cent since 2008. These procedures include nose jobs, boob jobs, bum lifts and tummy tucks: the trappings of celebrity and reality TV, rather than anything more traditionally fashionable. And this points directly to where the problem with body image really lies.

It's with trash TV and celebrity culture, and the magazines which run editorials of some D-lister in a string bikini whose body is the only real reason they have become famous. Rather than running classes in why one shouldn't aspire to look this way, why not run some kind of campaign to decrease the importance of all these blow-up dolls and bimbos? Why not offer a positive intellectual alternative to the cringy cosmetic culture of *TOWIE* and Katie Price?

Why not use the time spent teaching kids about body image to do something more constructive, something that will teach them there is life and success beyond your vital statistics? Body image classes will work the same way as basic reverse psychology, surely, and if we give anymore credence to the plastic lifestyle, we'll end up validating rather than vilifying it.

7 June 2012

⇨ This article originally appeared in The Independent and is reprinted with permission. Please visit www.independent.co.uk for further information.

Body image classes piloted in primary schools

With research showing that children are becoming dissatisfied with their bodies from a younger age, some schools are intervening and giving them ammunition to fight back. Katie Razzall reports.

How can you insulate children from the barrage of images of physical perfection? By age ten, research shows, one in five boys and one in three girls do not like the way they look.

Incredibly, ten is the average age children start dieting. There are all sorts of theories about why children are becoming dissatisfied with their bodies from a younger age, but in Bristol they're trying to give them the ammunition to fight back, with body image classes being piloted to some primary school children.

Channel 4 News spoke to some of the youngsters at St Peter's Church of England school in Bishopsworth, Bristol. After six lessons they had taken on board that what's on the inside of a person is much more important than what's on the outside. They were very knowledgeable about airbrushing and how the advertising industry markets unreal images to them.

Pressure to conform

One nine-year-old told me: 'I used to buy foundation, mascara, concealer and bronzer to cover up my freckles,' she said.

'After being taught body image and airbrushing, they said the ads aren't always true. Now I'm not spending money on make-up. You look nice anyway. To be honest, you don't look extra nice with make-up.'

It might surprise some people that a nine-year-old would buy make-up at all. But the pressures to conform are everywhere and there is a huge emphasis on image with children changing their pictures on social networking sites all the time.

Children as young as five are reported to be talking about diets, and now the Government has responded, saying these kinds of classes should be taught in all primary schools.

One of the teachers we met, Chris Calland, put it like this: 'It's our duty as educators to reflect what's happening in their lives. Unless we do it, they have no chance. By age 14 or 15 it's too late. If we build resilience early, it has more chance of working. We're giving them a fighting chance.'

6 July 2012

⇨ A version of this article first appeared at channel4.com/news and is reprinted with permission.

The impossible trend: look like Barbie

First recorded as popular in Japan, a new trend for young girls all over the world is hitting YouTube: to look like a Barbie doll.

By Elin Weiss & Hennie Weiss

The trend consists of applying make-up, doing one's hair, and dress in ways as to resemble a Barbie doll. Young girls and women are posting videos of themselves on YouTube in which they give advice on how to apply makeup and how to do their hair in order to look like Barbie dolls. This trend has apparently taken off and is becoming quite popular with certain girls being seen as the 'better Barbie' or more 'popular Barbie'.

There are also websites dedicated to teaching girls how to look like Barbie and tips on how to take care of one's body and hair in order to look more like the plastic doll. When searching the Internet it is easy for girls to find tutorials on how to master the look of Barbie and how to create 'Barbie hair' and how to achieve a 'Barbie face'.

It is troubling that young girls aspire to look like Barbie dolls. First off, we all know how much criticism the Barbie dolls have received for their anatomically incorrect and impossibly super slim bodies. Secondly, Barbie has also received criticism for promoting unhealthy body ideals and influencing young girls into believing that the Barbie body is common and attainable and more attractive than their own. This is a troubling thought since, according to a news article in *The Huffington Post,* Barbie's height (if she was a living woman) would be 5'9" tall, with and bust of 39", a waist that is 33", while she would wear a size three in shoes. Barbie would then weigh 110 lbs with a BMI of 16.24, which lands her in the BMI range of anorexic. Due to her anatomically incorrect body Barbie would have to walk on all fours. The same news article also stated that: 'Slumber Party Barbie was introduced in 1965 and came with a bathroom scale permanently set at 110 lbs with a book entitled *How to Lose Weight* with directions inside stating simply "Don't eat".'

One might think that young girls understand that Barbie's looks are unattainable and unrealistic, but do they really? This is not always the case. Some girls grow up to idolise Barbie to the point where they try to emulate her looks completely. Three real-life examples are UK women Sarah Burge and Charlotte Hothman, as well as American Cindy Jackson. Burge had more than 100 cosmetic surgeries in order to look like a human Barbie doll. Hothman has spent over £10,000, while Jackson spent more than $100,000 on cosmetic surgery. All three women stated that their obsession with the Barbie doll started when they were young girls, and that they have always wanted to look just like Barbie.

It is quite disturbing that this trend has surfaced among very young girls. It appears as if the obsession with appearance in young girls is getting more and more severe, especially now when some girls are attempting to attain a specific body weight and size that is constructed for non-human objects. It does seem as if the obsession with a certain appearance is indeed reaching younger and younger girls. It is important to care for one's health but an excessive fixation with one's appearance does seem unhealthy in regards to the expectations placed on these young girls. Since no person is perfect (and what is perfection anyway?) this type of fixation with beauty can probably only lead to unhappiness and body dissatisfaction in the long run.

There is tremendous diversity in terms of body size, shape, height and overall appearance among women. Some women are naturally very slim, some are very curvy, some have large breasts, some have smaller breasts, some are short and some are tall. In short, there is no limit to the ways that women look. What the Barbie ideal is perpetuating, however, is one type of body, one that is anatomically impossible, and one that is anorexic. Idealising the body of

Barbie also trivialises and glorifies the eating disorder anorexia, a disorder that millions of girls and women suffer from, and that many also die from.

It seems that the obsession with appearance and a certain type of beauty has gone so far as to now include the fixation with impossible to reach and inhuman beauty. Now more so than ever, young girls are on diets and are very unhappy about their body size and appearance. Many of these young girls are being taught that appearance and beauty are more important than any other characteristic or trait.

We find it inappropriate that young girls are being displayed this way on YouTube (even if they post these videos themselves) and we do believe that this new trend is damaging to young girls' self-esteem and body image since it promotes a distorted idealisation of the female body while perpetuating the notion that one's body is never good enough. Young girls should not be compared to dolls. Seeing the above facts make it even more disturbing that Barbie serves as the perfect ideal when it comes to girls and women's appearance.

18 April 2012

⇨ The above article originally appeared on The F-Word and is reprinted with permission. Please visit www.thefword.org.uk for further information.

Skinny bashing. Fat bullying. Image taunting. It's not OK...

If 'real/normal women' have curves, what does that mean for those of us who don't?

By Emma Woodhouse

Whichever end of the spectrum you're at and even if you sit happily, inconspicuously in the middle, you will almost certainly at some point in your life have been made to feel that you are somehow not good enough. The media may have perpetrated the myth that there is an ideal size, but it is we, the knowing public who continue to reinforce it, sometimes even when we think we're doing the opposite.

It is not right that we are being fed an unattainable image of the perfect woman who is all toned abs and glistening skin, the concept of spanx being only a kinky bedroom activity to the Adonis of the feminine body.

'It is not right that we are being fed an unattainable image of the perfect woman who is all toned abs and glistening skin'

But it is also not right that in the subsequent backlash, females who are all shoulders and elbows, tinny ribs and gangly legs are being made to apologise for how they look by the activists campaigning for more realistic body images.

'The sudden trend that compares pin-ups of the 1950s against modern 'image icons' [does] equally as much damage by targeting skinny girls'

The sudden trend that compares pin-ups of the 1950s against modern 'image icons' may have a valid point about the distortion of body image during the last century, but they do equally as much damage by targeting skinny girls.

I don't have breast augmentations or eating disorders. I don't do exercise. I don't expect anyone to feel 'sympathy' for me because I'm petite, but by the same token, I don't want to feel like my body or body shape is being devalued because of what it's not.

I have of course heard it all before: been told to eat some more pies, frequently quizzed on my assumed issues with food and even, on the eve of my wedding, been told by my own mother that I'm too skinny and need to put on weight. It sucks to be told you need to change, whether you're seven stone or 27 stone.

But that inverted snobbery is not my problem here. My problem with these types of images is the comparison. I fundamentally believe that we are not all meant to be identikit humans. We are all different shapes and sizes and I do not for one second believe that any one of those shapes and sizes is any better than the rest.

Whilst you might think you're crusading for a more acceptable 'ideal image' by reposting these wry little graphics, you're just hurting someone else along the way. You're fuelling the nasty, manipulative media message that we must compete to prove ourselves better than our sisters, friends and colleagues. You're making it worse.

The real crusade is learning to understand that there is no ideal image; there's just you. And me. And the other three billion women in the world.

'We as women have more than enough other issues to be dealing with, so how about we all just give each other a break?'

We as women have more than enough other issues to be dealing with, so how about we all just give each other a break and instead of genuflecting our issues to the opposite end of the spectrum, embrace our individuality and get on with our lives, regardless of what we look like? If you're a giant or a borrower, pigeon-toed or a hunchback, black, white, polka-dotted or otherwise, you are not more or less inferior to the next person. You are just different.

2 March 2012

This article formed part of a series entitled 'Laid Bare', that featured on a popular UK wedding blog {www. lovemydress.net}. The series was positioned to a demographic of fully grown women grappling with body issues during one of the most stressful/attention fuelled moments of their life.

Author Emma Woodhouse of The Wedding Reporter {theweddingreporter.co.uk} for Love My Dress {www.lovemydress.net}

⇨ The above article is reprinted with kind permission from Love My Dress. Please visit www. lovemydress.net for further information.

© *Love My Dress 2012*

British kids first consider surgery in their teens

Shocking new research has revealed that a quarter of British women surveyed first considered cosmetic surgery between the ages of ten and 15.

The 3,000 British women surveyed were aged between 18 and 30 years old and were asked at what age they first considered cosmetic surgery, to which 25 per cent of women answered between the ages of ten and 15 years old and 33 per cent said between the ages of 15 and 18 years old.

The survey conducted by One Poll shows a large number of women are considering plastic surgery from a very young age.

Paul Banwell, consultant plastic surgeon at Liberate Cosmetic Surgery, which funded the survey, said: 'There is no doubt that more and more younger people are considering cosmetic surgery and breast augmentation still remains the number one procedure. However, the statistics regarding the age at which women are first considering surgery is quite shocking.'

The survey, which asked British women how they felt about their appearance and their attitudes towards cosmetic surgery, also wanted to look at current trends and find out what young women know and don't know about surgery.

The research highlights the unhappiness many women and girls feel about their bodies.

In another study earlier this year, findings revealed that one in three women would be willing to trade at least one year of their life in order to enjoy their ideal body.

A team at the University of the West of England and the Succeed Foundation saw 320 British women questioned about their self-image.

The researchers found that, with 46 per cent of those polled having been bullied due to their appearance and four in five keen to lose weight, a significant proportion would be willing to go to extreme lengths to achieve their ideal figure.

More specifically, as well as being willing to shorten their life expectancy, nine per cent said that they would be willing to sacrifice the amount of time they are able to spend with a loved one, while 13 per cent would be happy to give up £5,000 of their annual salary to be in shape.

18 August 2011

⇨ Information from Adfero. Visit www.totallyliving.co.uk.

Dove launches campaign to support self-esteem programme

Dove, the Unilever-owned skin care brand, is launching its latest self-esteem initiative, with an ad campaign that encourages girls and women to have a positive relationship with beauty and themselves.

The campaign, created by Ogilvy & Mather, forms part of a £1.6 million drive and breaks on TV, supported by an on-pack promotion and in-store activity. The ads will carry the strapline, 'Together we can make a difference. Dove brings self-esteem education to girls'.

Ali Fisher, brand manager of Dove Skin, Unilever UK, said the brand hoped to create a 'step change' with the new campaign.

She said: 'At Dove, we are passionate about our social mission and want to continue our support to help young girls and women develop a positive relationship with their bodies.'

The 2012 Dove self-esteem programme aims to tackle women and girls' attitudes towards themselves, following research released by SIG, which showed 53% of girls in the UK have avoided certain activities because they feel bad about their looks.

The research also found that 22% of girls won't go to the beach or pool, while 20% have avoided physical activity or exercise, and one in ten will not go to the doctor.

Dove's self-esteem programme has previously run in schools, engaging with more than 800,000 people in the UK, and has invested £250,000 to run one-hour workshops in partnership with the Beat Eating Disorders Association. The brand aims to reach one million people by the end of 2012 through the new campaign.

23 March 2012

⇨ Information from Haymarket Publishing. Visit www.campaignlive.co.uk.

Girlguiding UK urges teenage girls to think twice about cosmetic surgery

Information from 24dash.com.

By Ellie Warfield

Today Girlguiding UK is responding to the shocking numbers of teenage girls considering cosmetic surgery by launching 'Give yourself a chance', an interactive digital resource offering tips to girls and young women urging them to consider alternative ways to boost self-esteem other than cosmetic surgery.

'Over one in ten girls aged 11–16 would consider cosmetic surgery to change the way they look'

Girlguiding UK has created 'Give yourself a chance' to tackle an issue highlighted in their ground breaking surveys of attitudes amongst girls and young women which found that:

⇨ 47% of girls think that the pressure to look attractive is the most negative part of being female;

⇨ 48% of young women aged 16–21 would consider cosmetic surgery; and

⇨ Over one in ten girls aged 11–16 would consider cosmetic surgery to change the way they look.

'Give yourself a chance' has already received the backing of the Girlguiding UK youth panel Advocate!, Campaign for Body Confidence, Mumsnet and BAPRAS, the British Association of Plastic, Reconstructive and Aesthetic Surgeons. Girlguiding UK are calling on teens to openly discuss the issue and to consider a range of alternatives to cosmetic surgery to help boost self-esteem.

'Give yourself a chance' is aimed at girls aged 12–16, who may not be members of the guiding movement. It is the latest initiative in Girlguiding UK's ongoing commitment to promote body confidence in today's girls and young women and is a useful tool for all adults to share with the girls and young women that they support.

Cathy Fraser Girlguiding UK spokesperson and head of Girlguiding UK's youth panel Advocate! said:

'Our research has shown the shocking extent to which girls would consider drastic action to change the way they look. Working closely with girls and young women, we are all too aware of the pressures they face to conform to a certain body image. "Give yourself a chance" encourages girls to boost their self-confidence without cosmetic surgery and to give themselves the opportunity to develop fully. Guiding can give young women the opportunity to build strong friendships, be challenged by new experiences and adventures, from geo-caching to international travel, and above all to accept themselves as they are.'

Lynne Featherstone, Minister for Equalities said: 'The constant pressure to look impossibly perfect, be like skinny celebrities and conform to imposed stereotypes is creating a rising tide of low self-esteem, depression and anxiety amongst young girls and, increasingly, boys. I want young girls to feel valued not because of what they look like but for what they can contribute and achieve. But this is not a job for government alone. Everyone has a role to play which is why I am delighted to lend my support to the 'Give yourself a chance' campaign which I think is an excellent and innovative way to reach young girls and tackle this modern-day virus which is undermining so many.'

Simon Kay, a plastic surgeon and member of the British Association of Plastic, Reconstructive and Aesthetic Aurgeons said: 'BAPRAS is pleased to support the Give yourself a chance campaign and fully endorses a policy of careful, considered and measured decision-making when it comes to cosmetic surgery. We encourage girls to take their time, discuss the issue with their parents or a responsible friend and to ensure a cooling off period before making any decision.'

To encourage teen girls to give themselves a chance, Girlguiding UK has worked with its young members and expert partners to develop a series of tips. Expert commentary has been provided by members of the Campaign for Body Confidence, BAPRAS and TV presenter Jayne Middlemiss. Aimed at teens, it also includes the experiences and testimonies of young people themselves in a bid to show other young women how to celebrate their bodies and enhance their self-esteem.

Try out lots of new things until you find something that you really enjoy whether it is running, cooking, climbing or writing. When you are feeling a bit down, do that activity and you will feel so much more confident about yourself. Liz, aged 21.

3 March 2011

⇨ The above information is reprinted with kind permission from 24dash.com. Please visit www.24dash.com for further information on this and other subjects.

Teenage modelling as a way to build confidence

Modelling is a great career path that can benefit a person in different ways personally and professionally.

If you are not sure if this is something you might be good at, there are a couple of ways to try it for a test run. You can contact a local professional photographer to see if he or she would like to do a test shoot with you. Some will even negotiate a trade agreement with you. If you have a photo-savvy friend that you would be comfortable working with, you can give that a shot too! Just doing a couple of shoots gives you the chance to try something in a controlled environment without fear of failure. You can learn about something new, and have all of the tools to be able to try it out. There is nothing wrong with trying and failing; there is only something wrong with not trying. You don't always want to wonder if modelling is for you!

As teenagers, many young people are faced with body image issues. Being a model at this age would mean that you are a person who others may look up to. Also, this profession or hobby gives you a good reason to stay in shape and stay healthy. Working as a model means that you have to look your best by eating healthy, exercising, and avoiding alcohol and drugs. These are good life lessons for teenagers to learn, and learning them as part of a career would make it that much easier to make the right decisions. If you are getting paid not to do something, that thing becomes easier to avoid. Therefore, things that you know are bad for you and bad for your body would be easier to avoid if you knew that doing them meant you would not get paid for the work that you do.

In addition to this, there are many advocates for modelling who say that it teaches teenagers positive qualities, such as public speaking and interaction with others. Everyone has seen that teenager who will not even take off the earphones when he or she is in the middle of checking out of a grocery store or spending time with family. This may not be a case of surliness, but a case of fear of not being understood or accepted as she is. Modelling is something that can help with this by drawing out the positive side of her personality, and teaching her to be something that she may not have the opportunity to learn otherwise.

Modelling is a great tool for young people for many reasons. They will be able to have a better self-image as a result of the work, and it will likely expose them to a variety of people, places, and experiences; making them all-round better people. It is not something that will just naturally come to you with no hard work, but it has a great payoff in the end, both monetarily and mentally.

⇨ The above information is reprinted with kind permission from How To Model Coaching. For more information on how to become a model please visit www.howtomodelcoaching. com. You can also visit www.mikelmurphy.com for information about the author.

© 2011 How To Model Coaching

Model Bethaney Wallace dies of anorexia aged just 19

A model who graced the cover of teen magazines has died of anorexia at just 19 years old.

Bethaney Wallace, who had suffered with an eating disorder for three years, was under 7 stone and too weak to work before her death.

She began modelling at just 12, being pictured in teen magazines *Make It Groovy, Popgirl* and *Girl Talk*.

Her father Clive told the *Daily Mail* the teen believed she was fat, saying: 'She would say she was fat but she was so beautiful – she didn't realise how beautiful she was. She had up days and down days. It was like Jekyll and Hyde.

'I tried to warn her that her organs would fail but she just said: "Don't be silly". If you mentioned food it would start an argument.'

Ms Wallace, from Newmarket, Suffolk, had been receiving medical attention but died in her sleep on 18 April at her grandmother's house.

Her father said before her death she appeared to have been making 'good progress' and had an eating plan. But her parents said doctors believed her heart had failed after being weakened by the disease.

Her mother Cathy said she had watched her daughter deteriorate in front of her, saying: 'You are slowly watching your child die.'

A spokesperson for eating disorders charity Beat said the illnesses took a 'huge toll on the body': 'Our hearts go out to Bethaney's family.

'Eating disorders are devastating illnesses and it is particularly

poignant that she had been making progress in her battle to beat her illness.'

Her death comes after a recovering anorexic called for airbrushed images in adverts aimed at children to be banned.

An inquest was opened and adjourned on 23 April.

1 May 2012

⇨ Information from *The Huffington Post.* Reprinted with kind permission from AOL (UK) Limited. Visit www. huffingtonpost.co.uk for further information.

Thinking about society's general portrayal of the ideal image of 'beauty' ...

Do you think that this is currently too thin, too large or about the right size?

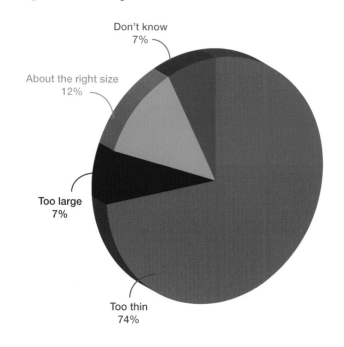

Don't know 7%
About the right size 12%
Too large 7%
Too thin 74%

Which one of the following would you rather have?

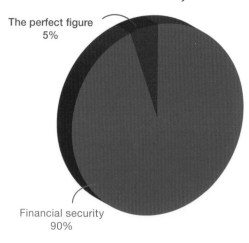

The perfect figure 5%
Financial security 90%

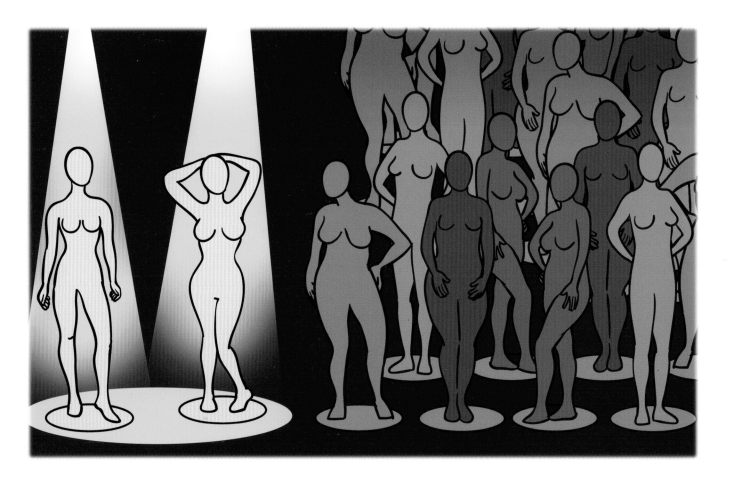

UN summit to discuss body image in media

Information from the Home Office.

Academy award winning actor Geena Davis has teamed up with Equalities Minister Lynne Featherstone to challenge the portrayal of women in the global media.

The minister is at a UN summit this week where she will host the first international event about body image.

'Every day, women across the world are surrounded by body images which bear little or no resemblance to reality'

She will join UN delegates on Wednesday 29 February to talk about how education can be used to battle negative body image and the UK's Body Confidence campaign, which focuses on gender stereotyping in the media and highlights how misleading images can cause stress on younger women.

Damage

The minister said: 'Every day, women across the world are surrounded by body images which bear little or no resemblance to reality, whether that be the "size zero" or the "perfect hourglass". These images can cause real damage to self-esteem.

'If children continue to grow up in a world filled with images of uniform beauty and airbrushed perfection, future generations will never be happy in their own skin. This is why I am bringing the debate to the UN.'

Body confidence

Last year the UK government launched the Body Confidence campaign to raise awareness about body image and encourage a more open and public conversation.

Geena Davis, founder of the Geena Davis Institute on Gender in the Media, welcomed the UK's body confidence campaign. She said: 'Hollywood and the media have the power to shift attitudes and achieve social change, particularly in how our children value themselves and each other. There is a real need to dispel the myths of the 'perfect' body that just don't match up to the real world.'

The body image event is one of a series of high level activities during the two week UN Commission on the Status of Women, which will cover a range of issues affecting women.

24 February 2012

⇨ Information from the Home Office. Visit www.homeoffice. gov.uk.

Rewarding diversity in magazines

Last Wednesday night the magazine publishing industry stormed the Grosvenor House Hotel for the PPA Awards 2012.

This major annual event is our opportunity to celebrate the people, teams and brands within the industry and, judging by some of the anecdotes the following day, there was no shortage of celebration among the winners and those who were highly commended for their hard work over the past 12 months.

This year, there were two new categories among the 22 awards handed out on the night: Front Cover of the Year and the PPA Diversity Award. Supported by equalities minister Lynne Featherstone as part of the Government's body confidence campaign, the PPA Diversity Award has been introduced as a celebration of diversity within the magazine publishing sector.

Given that every year 80% of the population spends around £2 billion across 3,000 consumer titles that cater for almost every demographic and specialist interest area you could imagine, there's diversity aplenty to celebrate in printed magazines. And that's not including the content on the websites of magazine brands and the increasing number of magazines downloaded onto tablet devices as digital editions.

For the PPA Diversity Award, however, the judges were specifically looking for examples of how magazine brands provide genuine representation of a diverse spread of people within their editorial content, reflecting a variety of body sizes and shapes, ages, sexualities and ethnicities.

The shortlist was in itself diverse, featuring leading women's titles such as *Cosmopolitan* and *ELLE* from Hearst Magazines UK, Centaur Media's business weekly *The Lawyer*, and Immediate Media Co's *Something Special* magazine, which has been created to be accessible for children with learning disabilities.

The independent judges said they were 'extremely impressed' with the overall high standard of entries. Competition was so close, in fact, that the panel made the decision to highly commend *Psychologies* magazine.

There could be only one winner, however, and it was *Essentials* magazine that took to the stage to accept the award from Equalities Minister Lynne Featherstone. Explaining why the IPC Media title should be singled out, the judges said: '*Essentials* really puts diversity into practice, clearing its front covers for unique portraits of real women. This is the title currently setting the standards for all other titles in this area.'

Essentials first published a Real Women special issue in 2010, marking the first time it had not used models or celebrities on its cover. The positive feedback prompted editor Jules Barton-Breck to make the decision to continue to use real women on its covers throughout 2011 and into 2012, reinforcing its tagline of 'No models, no celebs - just you!'

Commenting on the award win, Publishing Director Linda Swidenbank said: '*Essentials* has been steering a path of reflecting women in a celebratory way for a good few years now. Each month it brings this to the forefront with the reader cover star, drawing from a wide range of inspirational women across the UK.'

Hear, hear, Linda. Our thanks to Lynne Featherstone for her input into this inaugural award and congratulations again to Jules Barton-Breck and the *Essentials* team.

28 June 2012

⇨ Information from *The Huffington Post*. Visit www.huffingtonpost.co.uk.

Parent pack for child body confidence launched

A new guide for parents to help them educate children about how the media alter images and the impact this can have on self-esteem has been backed by Equalities Minister Lynne Featherstone today.

The body image parent pack, developed for six–11-year-olds by not-for-profit organisation Media Smart, marks the latest contribution to the Government's Body Confidence campaign.

'Explores how ideas about the "perfect" body have changed through the ages'

The pack encourages children to think about how and why images may have been altered and the effect this can have on their own body image. It also explores how ideas about the 'perfect' body have changed through the ages and offers tips for parents on how to talk to their child about the subject.

'Parents will be able to download materials – which include digitally enhanced pictures of celebrities – to help their children gain more realistic perceptions of the images they see'

Images in the media

Equalities Minister Lynne Featherstone said: 'Young people are being set an impossible standard by images in media and advertising which can erode their self-esteem.

'As parents, we are often aware of these issues, but may not have the advice and guidance we need to talk to our children.

'This will be an important contribution to the Government's body confidence campaign and I am delighted to have worked with Media Smart. I want the pack to empower parents to have those difficult conversations and open the door to discussion.'

This initiative follows the launch last year of a teaching pack for primary schools, which has since been downloaded by over 1,500 teachers across the UK.

Parents will be able to download materials – which include digitally enhanced pictures of celebrities – to help their children gain more realistic perceptions of the images they see.

Media Smart Chairman Paul Jackson said: 'We have been overwhelmed by the response we have had to the body image teacher pack, both in terms of the volume of responses and the enthusiasm with which it has been received. We have found that children respond really well when they realise that most of the images they see have been altered in some way and are aspirational but not realistic.

'Encourages children to think about how and why images may have been altered and the effect this can have on their own body image'

'Extending our schools' resources to include educational tools for parents will be an important step in helping as many children as possible think critically about the images they see around them every day, and we were delighted to work with Home Office Minister Lynne Featherstone to develop this resource.'

22 June 2012

⇨ The above information is reprinted with kind permission from the Home Office. Please visit www.homeoffice.gov.uk for further information on this and other subjects.

Key facts

- At the age of five, children begin to understand other people's judgement of them. At seven they're beginning to show body dissatisfaction. As adults, 90% of British women feel body-image anxiety, and many women in their 80's are still anxious about the way their bodies look. (page 4)

- Half of all 16- to 21-year-old women would consider cosmetic surgery and in the past 15 years eating disorders have doubled. (page 5)

- A famous study in Fiji showed that after television was introduced to the island for the first time in 1995, after three years with TV teenage girls who watched it were 50% more like to describe themselves as 'too fat'. 29% also scored highly on a test of eating-disorder risk. (page 5)

- Ben Barry, a PhD student at Cambridge University, surveyed 3,000 women the vast majority of whom 'significantly increase purchase intentions when they see a model that reflects their age, size and race.' (page 6)

- Rates of depression in women and girls doubled between 2000 and 2010; the more women self-objectify, the more likely they are to be depressed. (page 6)

- The Good Childhood Inquiry found that 10-15% of young people reported that they were unhappy with their appearance (Children's Society, 2012). (page 11)

- There are about one in ten children and young people with a mental disorder (Green, 2005), and about 1.6 million people in the UK are affected by eating disorders (Beat, 2004). (page 11)

- 30% of men surveyed have heard someone refer to their 'beer belly', 19% have been described as 'chubby' and 19% have overheard talk about their 'man boobs' (moobs). (page 13)

- 320 women studying at 20 British universities completed The Succeed Foundation Body Image Survey in March 2011. 46% of the women surveyed have been ridiculed or bullied because of their appearance. 39% of the women surveyed reported that if money wasn't a concern they would have cosmetic surgery to alter their appearance. (page 15)

- Central YMCA and the Centre for Appearance Research at the University of the West of England recently conducted a survey of 810 young people and 759 adults across the UK. The research reveals that at least one in four adults feel depressed about their bodies. Over half of the adolescent girls (54.1%) said that girls at their school have body image problems and about a quarter of boys (23.7%) think that boys have body image problems. (page 18)

- In the same survey almost three quarters of adults (70.6% of men and 80.9% of women) think that consumers are not aware of the extent to which images of people in the media have been airbrushed. (page 18)

- 40% of young adults have used, or asked someone else to use, airbrushing techniques to make a photo of themselves look more attractive. (page 24)

- According to a news article in *The Huffington Post*, Barbie's height (if she was a living woman) would be 5'9'' tall, with a bust of 39'', a waist that is 33'', while she would wear a size three in shoes. Barbie would then weigh 110 lbs with a BMI of 16.24, which lands her in the BMI range of anorexic. Due to her anatomically incorrect body Barbie would have to walk on all fours. (page 31)

- Out of 3,000 British women, aged between 18 and 30 years old, who were surveyed by One Poll and asked at what age they first considered cosmetic surgery, 25% of the women answered between the ages of ten and 15-years-old, and 33% said between the ages of 15- and 18-years-old. (page 33)

- Out of 3,000 British women asked for a survey funded by Liberate Cosmetic Surgery, the research revealed that 46% have been bullied due to their appearance and four in five were keen to lose weight, whilst a significant proportion would be willing to go to extreme lengths to achieve their ideal figure. (page 33)

- Girlguiding UK's survey has shown that 47% of girls think that the pressure to look attractive is the most negative part of being female. (page 34)

Airbrushing

A technique used to edit photos. Airbrushing may involve the removal of blemishes or spots, changing the shape or size of a person's features, and may lighten a person's skin tone. These digital edits are usually done in a way to make the final effect appear natural.

BMI

An abbreviation which stands for 'Body Mass Index' and is used to determine whether an individual's weight is in proportion to their height. If a person's BMI is below 18.5 they are usually seen as being underweight.

Body image

Body image is the subjective sense we have of our appearance and the experience of our physical embodiment. It is an individual's perception of what they look like or how they should look like. It can be influenced by personal memory along with external sources such as the media and comments made by other people.

Cognitive

A term referring to the mental processes of perception, memory, judgement and reasoning.

Cosmetic surgery

A medical procedure which changes a person's appearance and can be performed on most parts of the human body. Cosmetic surgery can involve procedures such as inputting breast implants, bum lifts, Botox and lip fillers as well as changing bone structure.

Eating disorders

People with eating disorders usually over-estimate their size and will eat less food than their body requires in order to lose weight or to maintain a low weight. Eating disorders include anorexia nervosa, bulimia nervosa along with binge-eating disorders and if they are not diagnosed properly they can lead to serious illness or even death.

Objectify/Objectification

To turn something into an object in relation to sight, touch or another physical sense. To 'objectify' a person means to turn them into an object, meaning that they do not possess the same human rights as another individual. The person objectified is usually dominated by another person, or group of people.

Photoshop

A term applied to photos which are edited using digital software, and usually refers to editing which is done using the computer programme Adobe Photoshop. Airbrushing is one technique which may be used when 'photoshopping' an image.

Rhinoplasty

A procedure involving cosmetic surgery which involves altering the size or shape of a person's nose. Commonly referred to as a 'nose job'.

Self-esteem

A term referring to how an individual feels about their body. Relating to self-confidence, if a person has low self-esteem they may feel unhappy with the way they look. Alternatively, if a person has good/high self-esteem then they may feel particularly confident about their appearance.

Size-zero

A term referring to U.S. clothing, size-zero is equivalent to a UK size-four. In order to fit into size-zero clothing an individual must have the waist measurement of 23 inches which is the average waist size of an eight-year-old.

Assignments

The following tasks aim to help you think through the debate body image and provide a better understanding of the topic:

1. Imagine you are an Agony Aunt writing for a national newspaper. A young girl has written to you admitting that she has self-esteem and body confidence issues. Write a suitable reply giving advice and information on where she may look for support in order to tackle her concerns.

2. Do you think male body issues receive as much media coverage and are as readily discussed as female body issues? Give reasons for your answer and consider which issues are frequently discussed for both genders, and/or what needs to be more discussed in your opinion.

3. Produce a poster using the statistics surrounding body image issues found throughout this book. You may also find the key facts section in this book useful.

4. Using news sites such as www.bbc.co.uk, find three articles which discuss issues concerning body image. What are the topics that come up and how do they engage with concerns raised in this book?

5. Produce a leaflet which raises awareness about the dangers surrounding eating disorders such as anorexia nervosa, bulimia nervosa and binge-eating disorders. You may find articles in 'Chapter 2: Body image issues' of use.

6. Hold a class discussion on body image to discover which concerns directly affect you and your fellow students. You may want to consider how images circulated in the media affect your self-confidence or consider whether any of the statistics found in this book are also applicable to your perception of yourself.

7. 'We hate how we look because of our new complicated visual culture, because of a fashion industry that has not adapted, a media that forensically analyses women's bodies and saturates our culture with body-change stories' (page 8). Do you agree?

8. Watch an episode of *Gok's Teens: The Naked Truth*. Write a review summarising the issues that are raised, how the teenagers featured on the programme suffer with body-confidence issues and what actions, if applicable, were taken to resolve these problems.

9. In small groups compile exercises for a workshop designed to advise and comfort those who suffer with low self-esteem and body confidence issues. You may want to use the exercises presented in the article entitled *Body image* (page 1) as inspiration.

10. Create a storyboard for a YouTube video explaining how airbrushing and Photoshop alter photographs. You should provide examples of digitally enhanced photos which are circulated by the media and you should discuss how these edited photographs may affect members of the public who see them.

11. As a class hold a debate on teen modelling. One half of your class should represent those in favour of teenage models and the other should represent the argument relating to the risks and implications of teenage modelling. Evidence for your respective arguments may be found in the articles entitled *Teenage modelling as a way to build confidence* (page 35) and *Model Bethaney Wallace dies of anorexia aged just 19* (page 36).

12. Write an article on the issues surrounding the possible impact that social media has upon body image and self-esteem. You should conduct some online research on the topic, investigating how viable this claim may be, as well finding evidence to support your conclusions.

13. Research the charity 'Body Gossip' and look at their videos and online interactive content. Produce a PowerPoint presentation which explains the work the charity does and how it engages with, and helps to reduce, body confidence issues.

14. 'Everyone is influenced by images that do not portray reality. For those young people whose sense of self worth is already low – this hyper perfectionism is toxic' (page 29). Discuss.

15. In pairs, discuss whether you think the Government is doing enough to tackle body image issues is children and teens. What else could they do? Does your school discuss these issues with you? Do you think they should? Make notes on your discussion and feedback to your class.

16. In small groups, design an app for a smartphone that will highlight the body image issues that teenagers today are facing. Your app should also offer help and advice on tackling these issues.

Acknowledgements

The publisher is grateful for permission to reproduce the following material.

While every care has been taken to trace and acknowledge copyright, the publisher tenders its apology for any accidental infringement or where copyright has proved untraceable. The publisher would be pleased to come to a suitable arrangement in any such case with the rightful owner.

Chapter One: What is body image?

Body image, © University of Dundee Counselling Service, *Uncomfortable in our own skin: the body image report*, © Guardian News & Media Ltd 2012, *Disturbing trend as schoolkids post videos asking strangers: 'Am I ugly?'*, © 2012 AOL (UK) Limited, *Body image inquiry*, © 2012 Young Minds, *Body image concerns more men than women, research finds*, © Guardian News & Media Ltd 2012, *30% of women would trade at least one year of their life to achieve their ideal body weight and shape*, © UWE 2012, *Beer belly is biggest body issue for men*, © UWE 2012, *I love me*, © Central YMCA, *Body image and mental health*, © 2012 Compass Youth.

Chapter Two: Tackling body image issues

All Party Parliamentary Group inquiry on body image, © Central YMCA, *Why responsible advertising to children should be top of the agenda,* © Guardian News & Media Ltd 2012, *'Pretty as a picture'*, © Credos 2011, *Health food magazine airbrush fattens up skinny model*, © Telegraph Media Group Limited 2010, *'Ban airbrushed photos aimed at teens,' says former anorexia suffered Rachael Johnston*, © AOL (UK) Limited 2012, *The debate: should body image lessons be introduced in schools?*, © The Independent, *Body image classes piloted in primary schools*, © Channel 4 2012, *The impossible trend: look like Barbie*, © The F-Word 2012, *Skinny bashing. Fat bullying. Image taunting. It's not OK...*, © Love My Dress 2012, *British kids first consider surgery in their teens*, © 2011 Square Digital Media Ltd, *Dove launches campaign to support self-esteem programme*, © Haymarket Business Media 1957 – 2012, *Girlguiding UK urges teenage girls to think twice about cosmetic surgery*, © 2012 24publishing, *Teenage modelling as a way to build confidence*, © 2011 How To Model Coaching, *Model Bethaney Wallace dies of anorexia aged just 19*, © AOL (UK) Limited 2012, *UN summit to discuss*

body image in media, © Crown copyright, *Rewarding diversity in magazines*, © AOL (UK) Limited 2012, *Parent pack for child body confidence launched*, © Crown copyright.

Illustrations:

Pages 3, 35: Don Hatcher; pages 9, 37: Angelo Madrid; pages 16, 38: Simon Kneebone.

Images:

Cover and pages i, 24: © svetikd; page 4: © selimaksan; page 14: © Sava Alexandru; page 23: © Asif Akbar; page 31: © Richard Newton; page 32: © kirsche222; page 39: © Kim Gunkel; page 41: © Micah Burke.

Additional acknowledgements:

Editorial on behalf of Independence Educational Publishers by Cara Acred.

With thanks to the Independence team: Mary Chapman, Sandra Dennis, Christina Hughes, Jackie Staines, Jan Sunderland and Amy Watson.

Cara Acred

Cambridge

September, 2012